A PRACTICAL GUIDE TO DIGITAL RESEARCH
GETTING THE FACTS AND REJECTING THE LIES

A PRACTICAL GUIDE TO DIGITAL RESEARCH

GETTING THE FACTS AND REJECTING THE LIES

MERCEDES K. SCHNEIDER

GARN PRESS
NEW YORK, NY

Published by Garn Press, LLC
New York, NY
www.garnpress.com

Book and cover design by Ben James Taylor

Library of Congress Control Number: 2019955575

Publisher's Cataloging-in-Publication Data

Names: Mercedes K. Schneider
Title: A Practical Guide to Digital Research: Getting the Facts and
Rejecting the Lies / Mercedes K. Schneider.
Description: New York: Garn Press, 2020. | Includes bibliographical
    references and index.
Identifiers: LCCN 2019955575 | ISBN 978-1-942146-78-0 (pbk.) |
    978-1-942146-79-7 (Kindle ebook)
Subjects: LCSH: Internet Research--Methodology. | Education--Re-
    search. | Internet Searching. | Educational Evaluation. | BISAC:
    EDUCATION / Research. | REFERENCE / Research. | EDUCA-
    TION / Reference. | EDUCATION / Computers & Technology. |
    EDUCATION / Education Policy and Reform / General.
Classification: LCC ZA4228.S357 2020 (print) | LCC ZA4228 (ebook)
| DDC 370.71--dc23.

Library of Congress record available at https://lccn.loc.
gov/2019955575.

*For my mother, Mary Louise Mills
Schneider, whose geese do not chase me
because I resemble her*

"There's no reason why, if efficiency experts put their minds to it, in the way they have to routing products in a factory, they couldn't figure out some scheme so a person wouldn't have to monkey with all this practicing and exercises that you get in music. ... I knew this correspondence school business had become a mighty profitable game....

... Always figured somebody'd come along with the brains not to leave education to a lot of bookworms and impractical theorists but make a big thing out of it."

--Real-estate agent George Babbitt to his son, in Sinclair Lewis' Babbitt.

TABLE OF CONTENTS

INTRODUCTORY REMARKS

This book chiefly concerns how to use the internet to conduct investigative research. Even as I regularly blog and write research-based books on education reform (ed reform), I teach full time, so the ability for me to conduct most of my investigations via the internet is critical to my producing writing based upon such queries. There are occasions in which what began as an internet search resulted in a face-to-face personal interview, and so I have included a short section on this "non-digital" approach. However, given my time constraints, such "off-the internet" personal interview research approaches are rare for me.

Being a teacher at heart, I also desire to assist others wishing to engage in their own chiefly-online research queries. Thus, the initial idea for this publication stemmed from my desire to equip parents and other community members to investigate the activities and spending of individuals and groups associated with market-based ed reform. However, once I completed my writing and considered the varied and numerous research lessons distilled in this book, I realized that what I had created was a practical, concise research guide useful to anyone seeking answers for any number of research inquiries, including students in high school and college, professionals, and community members. While the examples in this book are chiefly centered on my own research focus in ed reform, the experience behind the research renders this text a valuable tool for anyone desiring to competently investigate a variety of research situations.

As a trained researcher and former college professor of statistics and research, I realize that the very idea of research is often a daunting one, even to those who pursue advanced degrees. On multiple occasions, I have had graduate students cry in my presence at the very thought of completing formal coursework (computerized coursework, at that!) on research. Nevertheless, as I have told my students in the past, and as I assure readers now, there is no need to fear. You can conduct you own research, and you can do so more easily than you may realize.

I will do my best to make this journey both enjoyable and profitable.

My goal is to offer an easy-to-read, easy-to-digest, concise tutorial, and, as previously noted, one based upon my own experience as an investigator and writer about issues chiefly surrounding market-based, corporate-styled, ed reform. The ed reform movement has been notably sweeping the country in the past two decades at the expense and detriment of the traditional, local-board-operated community public school. This movement has resulted in the testing mania of grading students, teachers, and schools using standardized test scores, and the promotion and expansion of privately-operated, publicly-funded charter schools and publicly-financed, private-school-attendance-enabling educational vouchers. The corporate reform efforts have been in motion for longer than ten years, but I propose that these efforts have particularly come to a head with the passage of the No Child Left Behind Act of 2001.[1]

The examples featured here are intended to illustrate how I engage in researching a number of investigations that I have undertaken over the past seven years, amounting to well over a thousand blog postings and three books other than this one. Moreover, I remind readers interested in researching other areas that the skills, techniques, and sources referenced in this book are certainly not limited to any single research interest or to researchers working in one specific field.

A few words about the organization of this book. It is not divided into chapters as one might find in most books, but instead is primarily organized according to the research resources, techniques and skills that I found useful in tackling two general categories of queries—those centered on individuals, and those principally concerning organizations. Of course, this dichotomy is somewhat artificial because 1) the reality is that organizations are comprised of individuals, and 2) some research resources, skills and techniques are useful in researching both individuals and organizations. Despite this overlap, and aside from opening words about the value of original sources and guidance on where to begin, I decided that the most logical presentation was to divide the material into two sections, one centered upon my work in researching individuals, most of whom promote market-based, ed reform ideas, and one centered on organizations, most of which focus on advancing such market-based, corporate-styled, ed reform.

Finally, this book is not meant to be an intimidating, hyper-cerebral read. Far from it. It is meant to aid those with little to no research training in trying to uncover the manifestations of market-based ed reform in their own backyards, and, for those with a bit more research savvy and experience, it is intended to ideally sharpen and build on their experience. To those ends, this book is meant to be practical. I am simply passing my learning on to you, my readers, in a document pleasantly devoid of any over-starched rhetoric of academia. That noted, some research resources are by nature more technical than others. Therefore, to gain a better grasp of the content of some sections, such as those concerning nonprofit tax forms or campaign finance disclosures, readers may wish to access and view some of the resources linked in the end notes even as they read the associated sections.

One last note—my thanks to Freda Baine for reminding me that research always requires a context. Also, many, many thanks to Denny Taylor and the diligence of Garn Press for the investment in and enthusiasm about this book.

And so, let us begin.

THE IMPORTANCE OF ORIGINAL SOURCES

When I write, I make it a priority to secure and offer to my readers original documents critical to supporting my assertions. Not all online publications make their sources directly and immediately available to the public. Such a decision may be a matter of editorial convenience because sometimes it is easier not to provide live links in an online publication, or the referenced document might be too large to attach. If my reputation as a researcher/writer is on the line, I do not want some critical point in my work to be based on secondhand information, so I always make a serious effort to base my conclusions on original documentation. I also want my readers to be able to verify those conclusions via their own direct examination of the primary documentation itself if they so choose.

Though much of this book will involve advice and instruction on securing original sources necessary to solidly support one's assertions and conclusions, this does not necessarily mean that

I am able to begin a research query with an original source in hand. Sometimes this happens, but mostly not. I often base my writing on an article or a news brief that has already been publicized, so let's begin with such a scenario. Let's say that I read an article from a local or national paper and I want to verify the claims, which I find often leads to expanding upon the claims. If the news article I read includes a link to the original source of information, or itself is the original source as in the case of a firsthand interview, then locating original documentation requires little to no further effort.

However, I have noticed, for example, that news articles that reference litigation often do not link directly to the case file. Indeed, the article might not even provide the name of the case. Such was the situation when I wished to post about a Louisiana judge's ruling about a teacher's being forcefully removed from a local school board meeting.[2] I located local news coverage about the ruling itself, but it seemed that no articles linked to the actual judgment. And what complicated matters was that the judgment was only a few days old, which means that searching legal case law websites yielded no information.

To solve this issue of locating the case, I followed other links in local publications, one of which took me to a teachers' union Facebook page. The page happened to have a picture of the judgment. This discovery allowed me to procure the actual case title, court, judge, and docket number, all of which I began to search as keywords online. In turn, these actions led me to the union's press release in another source, and it was there that the entire judgment was available in a document that could be downloaded.

Had I still been unable to procure a downloadable version of the judgment, my backup plan was to include pictures of the judgment from the union Facebook page and type the text myself so that others might easily read it. This would not have been an ideal situation but still one that would have allowed me to offer readers a view of the original.

I have also encountered situations in which an original legal document was embedded in a news article. In such cases, clicking on the embedded document might allow one to view an enlarged version that includes the option of downloading the document as a PDF file. Such is the case in this 2014 article in *The Washington Post* on teacher tenure litigation.[3] Nevertheless, I have discovered in some cases that the option to download a PDF file requires a membership agreement to an auxiliary service. Before I rush to blindly sign up for such extras, I conduct a search of the case file using the actual case name, court, judge, case number, date, or some combinations of these, to see if someone else has already provided the document to the public. If not, I engage in a case search on a legal site, such as Justia. There is more information about legal case searches in the later section on Litigation.

In some situations, access to original documentation is either not possible or is difficult to accomplish, for example, due to barriers of accessibility either to individuals interviewed or verified transcriptions of such interviews. In these cases, if the secondary source is well-established and has a reputation of credibility, then I check to see if the reporting includes some part of it that can be verified. If so, I may use the source, based upon the logic that if part of what a reputable source offers is true, then that source has reaffirmed to me it is also being truthful and accurate without embellishment. Two examples readily come to mind. The first concerns a blockbuster interview with billionaire Bill Gates that *The Washington Post* journalist, Lyndsey Layton, published in June 2014.[4]

In the article based upon that interview, Layton included the assertion that two key individuals approached Gates in 2008 with the request that he bankroll the controversial education standards know as Common Core.[5] She did not include links to a transcript, but she is an established, reputable source, and she did include the entire video interview that she conducted with Gates—an interview that I transcribed in its entirety and published for my readers. I also used the Layton-Gates interview in one of my books, and since that usage was for a paying audience, I paid *The Washington Post* for the rights to use the interview, another point to which I will return later in this book. Since Layton was accurate on many other points and forthcoming with the actual interview, I concluded that her point about the 2008 meeting, though not otherwise directly verifiable, could also be trusted.

A second example of extending faith in the veracity of a published assertion based upon the ability to verify related information concerns the anticipated 2019 resignation of White House press secretary, Sarah Huckabee Sanders. On June 13, 2018, CBS News published an exclusive article to the effect that both Sanders and her assistant, deputy press secretary, Raj Shah, were planning to leave the White House in 2019.[6] CBS's account was based on insider information, which leaves readers in the precarious position of judging the authenticity of the information. In this case I immediately considered the source, CBS News, which is an established news outlet with a long-standing, solid reputation. I also considered CBS's point that in her response to their report, Sanders deflected without directly denying the news.

Still, before reporting on this news, I allowed time to pass. Six months later, in December 2018, *AlterNet*, another national source not as solidly established as CBS but still with a good national reputation, reported that Sanders was hoping to exit but that she could not find another position and was therefore remaining at the White House at the outset of 2019 for want of a viable next career move.[7]

Two issues lend credibility to *AlterNet's* reporting—the previous reporting by CBS, and the inclusion of evidence that Shah planned to leave soon. In its December 2018 reporting, *AlterNet* pointed out that Shah had removed his White House job title from his Twitter bio, information that I could easily verify by viewing archived screen shots of Shah's Twitter bio (more to come on viewing web archives). I was also able to confirm that Sanders, despite posting on Twitter since the publication of the *AlterNet* article, had offered no denial of the report.

Therefore, since I was able to verify the changes in Shah's Twitter bio as asserted in *AlterNet*, and since the information in *AlterNet* was supported by CBS's previous reporting, *and* since Sanders offered no denial of the *AlterNet* report, I concluded that *AlterNet's* insider information about Sanders' desired exit was probably accurate. Even so, in an effort to underscore to my readers that I could not absolutely verify Sanders' position, I used the term "allegedly" in my own reporting. As it turns out, President Trump announced Sanders' resignation as White House press secretary via Tweet on June 13, 2019,[8] one year to the day after CBS published its story about Sanders' expected departure.

WHERE TO BEGIN?

In the previous section, I assumed that readers had a sense of where to begin a deeper dive into a search for original documentation after seeing a topic of interest already broached in media accounts. Of course, it is also possible that a parent or community member wishes to know more about an individual, organization, or situation due to personal interest aside from media coverage and is at a loss concerning how to proceed. The question then becomes, where does one begin such investigation?

Well, the first step is to conduct an online search for any published information on that person, organization, or situation. It might seem like common sense that interested individuals would automatically do such a search, but this is not always the case. People who are caught up in the distresses of community disruption or who feel blindsided by ed reform or another troubling discovery might succumb to a paralysis of helplessness, so to speak, and not necessarily think to calm themselves down and approach the situation methodically. So, advising people to start by searching the internet for what might already be available is worth emphasizing.

However, there is another lesson here—how to conduct an internet search effectively based upon keyword selection. Keyword selection is critical to an effective internet search, an issue that readers will see time and again throughout this book as I offer examples of my own research. Moreover, in addition to a frequent focus on effective keyword searches, I will discuss other useful research tools and techniques at points in the book where it seems logical to introduce them.

RESEARCHING INDIVIDUALS

Often what is of interest to one researching ed reform or other "movements" is discovering information related to individuals, such as their professional background and associations, attitudes and actions that drive decisions affecting the public, funding sources and applications, and the veracity of some promoted public image. In my research, I often have one or more of these discovery goals in mind. What I offer in this section on individuals chiefly concerns both those promoting ed reform and those affected by it. As such, I will provide a number of examples of individuals I have researched and written about, as well as my own research processes and the sources of information I accessed in conducting my research. My ultimate goal is to teach by dissecting and detailing my own examples, offering such for analysis by researchers both in the field of education and beyond.

Some of the sources I discuss in this section on researching individuals I also use when researching organizations, so readers should expect some overlap in information sources in both sections. Also, since organizations are comprised of individuals, researching an individual might lead to or otherwise coincide with researching an organization. As I noted previously, the dichotomy of researching individuals vs. researching organizations is a somewhat artificial separation and is adopted to provide some organization to this work. That noted, I have researched so many individuals and organizations that I am able to select examples that minimize confusion for those endeavoring to learn from my research methods and approach.

Let us begin examining my work on researching individuals in ed reform with the case of Eva Moskowitz.

An influential education reform presence in New York is former city council woman and Success Academy charter schools CEO, Eva Moskowitz. Moskowitz has been involved in ed reform for well over a decade, and she has a history in politics, as well. Thus, the keywords "Eva Moskowitz" will yield an overwhelming number of results. If I just wanted some general information on Moskowitz, merely searching her name might serve my purpose, and I could simply start reading some of the search results. However, let's say that I just learned about charter school co-location in New York City (NYC)—a situation in which NYC traditional public schools are being overtaken by charter schools that "co-locate"—

and I am interested in Moskowitz's activities in school building takeovers because I have heard that a legislator in my state is trying to promote a similar model for my city. In this case, a keyword search option is to combine the terms, "Eva Moskowitz co-location." However, since the NYC charter school co-locations have been happening for years, the number of search results may well continue to be overwhelming.

Since I want some inside information on the history of Moskowitz and how she has previously approached charter school co-location, in my keyword search, I need to connect her name to another term that will more efficiently yield search results focused on that history. Now, I could search, "Eva Moskowitz charter co-location history," and if I scroll down the results pages, I start to see articles from years ago on Moskowitz and her schools. I could begin perusing these articles to see if they have what I want—detailed, inside information on Moskowitz's approach to expanding her schools via co-location. Let's say that I do this and I find bits of information but not exactly what I am searching for. My goal in reading results from the current search is twofold, to find what I am looking for and to find keyword ideas for a more streamlined search.

Effective researchers always approach internet searches with both ideas in mind—finding what they are seeking or finding the next search lead by tailoring their keywords.

Let's say that in reading the results of my "Eva

Moskowitz charter co-location history" search, I discover that Moskowitz had a close relationship to then NYC schools chancellor, Joel Klein, who has been a key player in advancing Moskowitz's charter school expansion goals.

Thus, my next keyword search involves combining their names, "Eva Moskowitz Joel Klein." Via that search I discover the March 01, 2010, *Chalkbeat* article, "We Read the Moskowitz/Klein Emails So You Don't Have To."[9]

No source provides inside information like communications that the people involved assume will be private at the time that the communications are initially written. For that reason, emails among public officials are a fantastic source to capture public officials' genuine thoughts and intentions.

Even though the *Chalkbeat* article summarizes the key points in 77 pages of Moskowitz-Klein emails, the article also includes direct links to its original sources—the emails themselves.

EMAILS

Since my goal involved conducting thorough research on the Moskowitz-Klein exchange, I wanted to read the emails myself. *Chalkbeat* has already conveniently provided them, but had it not, I would have emailed the author of the article. Many authors include contact information either at the beginning or conclusion of their writing.

Such is true in this case.

What one is able to glean from Moskowitz's email exchange with Klein is exactly what excellent research uncovers—the story at its foundation, including a detailed unfolding of events and the shaping of the person, or event, or situation, as captured in reliable documents. Those 77 pages of emails between Moskowitz and Klein reveal Moskowitz's personality, attitudes, thoughts, actions, and interactions as she sought to expand her Success Academy charter schools in NYC.

Of course, Moskowitz's efforts to multiply her charter schools extend beyond 2010, the date of the referenced *Chalkbeat* article. However, once a researcher has a sense of Moskowitz and her relentless charter school expansion ambitions by closely reading the 77 pages of Moskowitz-Klein emails, that researcher has established a reliable foundation from which to critically appraise other writings about Moskowitz. This will then assist the researcher in not only selecting other research avenues to pursue, which might include public records requests for additional Moskowitz emails to NYC officials, but also in deciding how to advocate for the situation that led to interest in investigating Moskowitz in the first place.

My deep dive on and dissection of the referenced Moskowitz-Klein emails is described in my book, *A Chronicle of Echoes*, chapter 2: "Eva Moskowitz: Stage Mother of Charter School 'Success.'"[10]

EMAILS OBTAINED VIA PUBLIC RECORDS REQUEST

In the case of my research based upon the Moskowitz-Klein email exchange, the emails had been provided to me because *Chalkbeat* had already submitted a public records request to the New York State Education Department (NYSED) for those emails. Individuals holding public office or other government jobs and utilizing email in association with that public office or government job should expect that their correspondence may be subjected to public records requests at both the state and local level, or Freedom of Information Act (FOIA) requests, a term generally reserved for public records requests at the federal level.[11] This is one way in which those paid using public money can be answerable to the public.

Though it is possible that a member of the public might wish to submit a public records request for emails of a public servant working in another state, I find that since many people have a chief research interest in what is happening locally, it is more likely that the individual making the request lives in the same state and not another state. In the case of the Moskowitz-Klein emails, *Chalkbeat*, the New York publication submitting the request, made the results of the request available to the greater national and even international public.

I have submitted out-of-state public records requests for state education contracts (more to come about this) and have had my requests honored. In the age of online communication, it is relatively easy to honor such out-of-state requests across the miles, but it is also possible that state and local agencies might only honor the requests of taxpayers in their states. Both in-state and out-of-state requests might entail an administrative fee from the person making the request, and fulfillment of the request might require the requestor traveling to a state or local agency to view the documents in person, or fulfillment might entail copying documents, either on paper or CD-ROM, for example, and mailing them.

If one is interested in certain emails written by public employees using their work email accounts, the place to begin is to first identify the public agency where the individual is employed. Many of my public records requests are for email communications involving individuals employed at the Louisiana Department of Education (LDOE). Among its contact information, the LDOE website includes an email address, a brief word about submitting a records request by email, an expected time frame in which the request should be acknowledged, and a number to call if three days passes without acknowledgement.[12] However, if I wished, I could also locate public records information by Googling the entity name and including "public records request."

In making the request, the more precise and manageable the request, the better. For example, in April 2018, I was investigating the handling of special education data, namely, arrangements made out of the public eye for the transfer of LDOE special education data to SPEDx, an education company that already had a questionable relationship with the Texas Education Agency.[13] In my research, four officials of interest surfaced:

1. LDOE superintendent John White,
2. LDOE special education policy director, Jamie Wong,
3. LDOE data governance and privacy director, Kim Nesmith, and
4. SPEDx founder and CEO, Richard Nyankori.

I was also able to narrow the dates of interest and the specific interactions among the four officials to two requests:

1. Emails between Nyankori and Wong from 12/01/16 to 03/08/18, and
2. Emails among Nyankori, John White, and Kim Nesmith from 11/01/01 to 03/08/18.

The request still took some time to process because I asked for email correspondence across 15 months and 5 months, respectively.

In the end, the request yielded information that I was able to put in the public purview, including Nyankori's subcontracting with other business entities and sharing Louisiana special education student data with these entities, as well as his requests for data that LDOE officials could only access via a subcontractor. And more importantly, I was able to link to all of the emails resulting from my request and make the actual emails available to my readers.

EMAILS OBTAINED VIA FIRSTHAND CONTACT

Aside from utilizing emails already posted in news articles and those resulting from my own public records requests, a third manner in which I obtain email correspondence with individuals of research interest is to create firsthand email communications myself by contacting the individual. The use of direct contact is particularly helpful when there is no public record available because the information is either too precise or not directly associated with taxpayer-funded appointment/employment.

When I was working on my book, *Common Core Dilemma*,[14] I wondered whether the participants in the Common Core work groups were so publicly quiet about their experiences, and particularly whether they had any misgivings or reservations about their experiences, because they had signed confidentiality agreements. So, in April 2014, I located as many email addresses of those individuals as possible and sent a mass email identifying who I was via my ed reform research background. In my email, I asked one yes-or-no question, "Were you required to sign a confidentiality agreement regarding Common

Core work group discussions?"

When I email an individual for information that the person might perceive as controversial, if for no other reason than my position as someone writing in opposition to what that person is promoting, I think it is important for me to include in my initial email three components:

1. A brief yet clear identification of who I am, including reference to my work opposing market-based ed reform,
2. A brief statement for my purpose in writing, and
3. Short and simple inquiries stated in as neutral, unaccusatory, and respectful a manner as possible.

I do not want the person I am contacting to feel deceived because I concealed my identity and my research focus. I also believe I am more likely to receive an answer or begin an email exchange if my inquiries are brief and inoffensively worded.

I had one respondent who cautiously engaged in an email exchange with me and whose responses were very telling by the words he/she used in those responses. The respondent, who did not recollect signing a confidentiality agreement, did not give me permission to interview him/her "in a public forum because it is not the right time," which I found an intriguing response for its skittishness. I reference the email exchange in chapter 5 of *Common Core Dilemma*,[15] and I chose not to identify the individual because there was no need to either break that trust or put my publisher in a precarious position for "calling out" this person.

Sometimes the purpose of my email exchanges is to glean professional information that should be readily available on a key individual in the ed reform or other arena, but for some reason is not. I find this situation to be true of those establishing careers in ed reform and who have limited or even no certified teaching experience in the K12 classroom.

I discovered Education Trust founder Kati Haycock to be one such person. When I was researching Haycock's positions on federal education standards for *Common Core Dilemma*,[16] I could find no readily-available bio in which Haycock clearly delineated the degrees she held, including degree type, year of graduation, and field, although I did later find one such document. So in June 2014, I emailed her a request for what should have been easily-accessible professional background information on Haycock's bio page on the Education Trust website.[17] My request was to the point, "I am seeking specifics on college degrees earned by Kati Haycock—degree type, year of graduation, and field. Thank you." In this case, I felt no need to offer details on myself since a person promoting herself as "one of the nation's leading advocates in the field of education"[18] should offer comprehensive professional bio information to back up the claim.

Haycock responded with a single word, "For...?"

I chose to offer the purpose of my request and a link to my own background in my response:

> I have written a book on the history, development, and promotion of Common Core (to be published by TC Press in April 2015), and I discuss Ed Trust (NCLB support, ADP).
>
> I would like to include your education as part of your credentials, but your publicized bios do not include info on your degrees.
>
> So, I thought I would ask you directly.
>
> Thank you,
>
> Mercedes Schneider
>
> http://deutsch29.wordpress.com/about/

Haycock did respond with her own post-secondary education background. "Sure. Have Bachelors in Political Science from UC Santa Barbara and Masters in Education Policy from UC Berkeley." Through this exchange, I was able to confirm firsthand that Haycock holds no degrees in K12 classroom teaching, and like many ed reformers, her own education is removed from the very classrooms she influences. (See chapter 4 of *Common Core Dilemma* for my reference to this email exchange.[19])

Let us now turn our attention to a second example of direct contact via email.

In October 2013, I was interested in learning exactly how much classroom teaching experience American Federation of Teachers (AFT) president Randi Weingarten possesses. Though Weingarten is the president of a teachers' union, her actions often place her on the side of ed reform, including:

1. Accepting money from the Gates Foundation to promote the Common Core State Standards,[20]
2. Writing a foreword to Doug Harris' book on value-added modeling (VAM),[21]
3. Endorsing notoriously anti-traditional-public school candidates like Andrew Cuomo for reelection,[22] and
4. Even engaging in a robocall for Cuomo's running mate on the eve of the election.[23]

And like the bios of some market-based ed reformers, Weingarten's bio was questionably sketchy on her classroom teaching experience. At the time, I was blogging and also preparing my first book *A Chronicle of Echoes: Who's Who in the Implosion of American Public Education,*[24] for its April 2014 publication. However, my information on Weingarten's classroom teaching experience was nebulous at best, and I could find no comprehensive professional bio information on the decades-long leader of the US's second largest teachers' union, a dearth that is often a hallmark of wishing to avoid the subject.

So, on October 14, 2013, I contacted Weingarten directly via email to ask her about the specifics of her classroom teaching experience. Note that I clearly identified myself and my purpose for writing. Note also that my tone was polite and that I clearly operationalized "full-time." Given that the president of a teachers' union did not openly provide the number of full-time years she spent as a classroom teacher, I expected that she might try to evade offering an unambiguous response. Thus, my goal in writing was to be respectful but direct:

> Randi, my name is Mercedes Schneider. I have written a book on education reform and am in the process of editing.
>
> In my book, I refer to your teaching experience at Clara Barton High School. Your AFT bio only notes that you taught history and were there from 1991 to 1997.
>
> Not much info.
>
> In this email, I am seeking just a bit more detail.
>
> When people ask me about my teaching experience, my short answer is that I am in my 19th full-time year, with a couple of part-time years.
>
> I taught 5 years at the university, so I am in my 14th full-time year as a public school teacher. By "full-time," I mean that I am at school from first bell to last, five days

a week, and that I teach a full load-- the majority of my full-time day at school-- approx. 75% of my day.

Given my "first-to-last bell, full load" definition of "full-time," could you please tell me how many of your six years you taught full-time at Clara Barton?

I have used electronic media to ask of others their assistance in clarifying information for my book; I have directly quoted from their electronic responses as I plan to do with your response. I wanted to let you know so up front.

Thank you.

Mercedes Schneider

Career teachers do not require extensively parsed definitions to determine how many years they have been teaching. Weingarten used her first response to deflect and perhaps to buy more time. However, the fact that she could not or would not answer succinctly and to the point told a tale of wishing to conceal the response I was seeking. Below is Weingarten's response, dated October 26, 2013:

Sorry Mercedes I never saw this... What is a full university load.... How many periods a week.

I am not sure I know how to do the conversion for you, but I will try to piece it together this weekend. Most of my records are in storage and I don't have quick access to them.

Weingarten did not confirm that the six-year span of 1991-1997 that she allegedly spent teaching history at New York's Clara Barton High School was indeed a six-year, full-time teaching stint. Had those years been spent teaching full-time, there should have been no need for Weingarten to "piece together" this information.

My October 26, 2013, email exchanges with Weingarten continued with her questioning my sources, when the entire point was to receive accurate, firsthand information from her. I could not find any referenced, solid, official, confirmable information or even any secondary sources, and I was attempting to glean information from my email exchanges with her to illuminate exactly how long she had spent in the role of classroom teacher at Clara Barton High School. It seemed that she was there only six months. On October 26, 2013, I sent the following inadequately-referenced information from Wikipedia to Weingarten in hopes that she would correct any inaccuracies. Note that I again kept the tone of my emails professional and the content brief and to the point:

Randi, this is from Wikipedia, but the links do not substantiate the info. One of the references is the Village Voice article:

From 1991 until 1994 she taught on per diem basis 122 days over the period at Clara Barton High School in Crown Heights. In fall of 1994 she taught history full-time at the school.[5][7][14][15] By 1995, after six months of full-time teaching, Weingarten was elected Assistant Secretary of the UFT. [16][17] She continued teaching per diem, from 1995 to 1997.[18]

http://en.wikipedia.org/wiki/Randi_Weingarten

--M

The *Village Voice* article referenced above is the May 13, 2003, article, "Weingarten's War," written by Wayne Barrett. Below is article content that indicates Weingarten did not spend even a single year as a full-time teacher at Clara Barton High School:

In urging [New York City chancellor Joel] Klein "to walk in the shoes of teachers" on Saturday, she described how she'd done it, claiming that she "taught, sometimes full-time, sometimes part time, at Clara Barton High School for six years." Actually, records reviewed by the Voice indicate that she taught 122 days as a per diem teacher from September 1991 through June 1994, roughly one in four days. She then did what she told the Voice was her only full-time term in the fall semester of 1994, followed by 33 days as a per diem teacher in the spring of 1995.

Strangely, while she told the Voice she was a per diem for the 1995-96 and 1996-97 school years, her records list her as a full-time teacher. Because she was credited with the required two years of full-time service she doesn't even claim she performed, she was given a permanent certificate in September 1996. She has been on union leave since 1997, accumulating a total of nine years of pensionable city time though she only did one semester of full-time teaching.[25]

The problem here was that Weingarten was promoting a lie via sleight of information. I could not get a straight answer out of her. We exchanged emails several times on October 26, 2013, but each exchange yielded no clear response, which was telling in and of itself. Even so, she was willing to engage, and my goal was to persist by offering publicized information of her classroom experience so that she might set the record straight if indeed the heretofore publicized information were incorrect on any point.

In one of our many October 26, 2013, email exchanges, Weingarten wrote, "…I taught for six years, mostly part time, with 1 or 2 or 3 classes and one semester full-time…." As it was the clearest statement of Weingarten's actual teaching experience in a firsthand record, I included this direct quote as part of chapter 22 of *Chronicle of Echoes* ("The Aspen and Pahara Institutes: Advancing Privatization in Fine Style").[26] In the chapter I include examination of Weingarten's decision to engage in a discussion about teaching with Walter Isaacson, then chair of the ed reform organization, Teach for All, the international branch of Teach for America (TFA), at the 2012 Aspen Ideas Festival. In that videoed discussion, Weingarten ironically sounds like many TFA alumni who try to leverage their temporary classroom stints to make them seem equivalent to the teaching experience of authentic, full-time career classroom teachers.

I am convinced that the reason it took several email exchanges to glean even that little bit of information from Weingarten regarding her classroom experience was that she knew that her responses offered a written record of our discussion, and written records are powerful. Even evasive or false responses make for authentic written records, and it would have been dangerous for Weingarten to offer false information.

What is important to note is that my requests were carefully written, and they were respectful, objective, and remained on point. A respectful, objective, pointed request keeps the request itself from interfering with the quality and delivery of the information sought. No one reviewing my emails to Weingarten could rightly accuse me of trying to shape her response to suit any agenda.

Although I entered our email exchange with doubts as to her having taught even one complete school year full-time, first bell to last bell, five days a week, I was willing to be corrected on that point. In the end, obtaining accurate information must be the ultimate goal of any research quest, not shaving and shaping a preferred, slanted narrative.

TEACHING CREDENTIAL LOOKUP

One means for obtaining objective information regarding Weingarten's classroom teaching experience involves viewing her New York State teaching license. Many states offer to the public a "teacher credential lookup" search engine, and I have found that as the years pass, increasingly more states do so. New York happens to have such a search engine available,[27] and by using it, I was able to confirm that from 1991 to 1996, Weingarten held three temporary teaching certificates, at which time she was issued a permanent teaching certificate for social studies in grades 7 to 12. Ironically, Weingarten was not issued a permanent teaching certificate until the year before she permanently exited the classroom.

Those conducting research in other fields might wish to investigate whether a given profession of interest offers a credential search engine, the source of which could be some governmental or other professional society or agency.

In order to use the teacher lookup search engines, one must know both the state in which a teacher holds or should hold a teaching certificate, as well as the legal name of the person as it is recorded on the teaching certificate. Discovering such information can require a little sleuthing. In some cases, I have searched for the names of women prior to their marriage by Googling the known name and "marriage" or "wedding."

In Weingarten's case, it was easy enough to ascertain New York as the state in which she taught. Had I not known as much, I could have used the information provided in Weingarten's bio sketch regarding the name of the school (Clara Barton High School) and Googled the school name to discover that it is located in Brooklyn, New York. I should note that using school names alone to discover the state in which the school is located becomes more complicated if many schools nationwide have the same name. In such cases, investigating the residential history of the individual of interest might prove more fruitful. Note that this can become complicated if, for example, a person resides near a state line and lives in one state while teaching in another.

To determine if I could look up a New York teaching certificate, I Googled, "new york teacher certification lookup," and discovered that such a search engine exists for public use. However, when I searched for "Randi Weingarten," my search produced no result. Now some might be quick to say, "Aha! I knew she held no teaching certificate!" Be careful not to run headlong into false conclusions. My next move was to search by last name only, which yielded roughly 50 hits, none of which had a first name of Randi.

So I needed to find out if Weingarten's first name was something other than "Randi." In this case, I stumbled upon the information by accident in October 2013 when reviewing references in other articles about Weingarten's classroom teaching experience. I learned then that Weingarten's legal first name is Rhonda, and it is under "Rhonda Weingarten" that she is registered to teach in New York State. In Weingarten's case, online documentation noting her legal first name is virtually nonexistent. I use "virtually" because in order to locate such documents, I would have had to know Weingarten's first name was Rhonda to conduct the search.

If I had not already known her legal first name, I could have asked Weingarten herself via email, or asked one of her long-time colleagues. Or, and this would have taken some effort, I could have looked at the teaching credentials for all of the Weingartens in New York starting with those in Brooklyn to rule out dates that did not match, and then reduced my search to dates that corresponded to 1991–1997, the years Weingarten herself advertised as her years in the public school classroom. Though tedious, such a method would have drawn my attention to the licensure entry for "Rhonda Weingarten," at which time I could have worked backwards, so to speak, by Googling

"Rhonda Weingarten" to discover that "Rhonda Weingarten" and "Randi Weingarten" are one and the same.

Let us consider another example of utilizing a state's teacher certification lookup, this time from Louisiana. The individual of interest is a Teach for America (TFA) alumnus who was reputedly overseeing all teacher evaluations for the state, Molly Horstman.

Around 2011, notable turnover began at the Louisiana Department of Education (LDOE), with a number of TFA alumni assuming paid positions in LDOE, the most visible of these being the state superintendent, John White. One of the ways to confirm state education department employment is to submit a public records request for a complete record of all individuals employed by the state education agency, including job title, date of hire, and salary. By consulting such a listing that resulted from a public records request submitted by a colleague, I was able to confirm in part some news that friends had told me, that an individual by the name of Molly Horstman was employed by LDOE.

Horstman preceded White to LDOE.[28] By 2012, she was using the title of "director of Compass at the Louisiana Department of Education,"[29] COMPASS being Louisiana's state teacher evaluation system.[30] The problem with Horstman's being in charge of a statewide teacher evaluation system was her temporary stop as a TFA classroom teacher. Of course, advertising oneself as the director of Louisiana teacher evaluations begs the question of the validity of one's own credentials, which is where the Louisiana teacher certification search engine[31] came in handy.

Unlike the situation with Rhonda "Randi" Weingarten, Molly Horstman's teaching credentials were easy to locate since her last name is not a common name in Louisiana and since neither her first nor her last name had changed. (More to come on investigating name changes.) What I gleaned in reading Horstman's Louisiana teaching certificate was:

1. She had only graduated from college five years earlier, in 2007,
2. She completed an alternative teacher certification program in 2008 while already holding a one-year, provisional teaching certificate granted in 2007,
3. She was issued a three-year provisional teaching certificate which had expired in 2011, and
4. Horstman herself had never undergone the necessary teacher evaluation to renew her own teaching certificate.

In March 2013, I wrote about Horstman's situation,[32] which she had already tried to downplay in the media in September 2012 in a Baton Rouge *Advocate* article that referenced her lack of classroom experience and expired teaching certificate,[33] and which was likely the initial source of information on Horstman communicated to me by my colleague. In blogging about Horstman, I was able to add to what was already in the news by adding links by which the public could verify my sources, one of which involves Louisiana's publicly-available, teacher certification lookup. I was also able to chronicle the blowback White received for having Horstman as "director" of teacher evaluation and his subsequent backpedaling. Horstman left LDOE in 2013.[34]

LINKEDIN

Another excellent place to begin researching an individual is to conduct a keyword search of that individual via the online bio site, LinkedIn. One can do so in limited fashion without joining the site. However, I have found that as the years passed, I was accessing LinkedIn so often that the site required me to join in order to continue. I was able to do so by providing minimal personal information. Some colleagues like using LinkedIn as a means of professionally connecting, but I am not at that point yet. Perhaps in the future I will post a more thorough bio on the site.

LinkedIn is an excellent site for researching the education and employment histories of many professionals, including those promoting corporate-styled ed reform. It seems that pro-education reform individuals value the site and therefore choose to post detailed information about their professional lives. Moreover, what I have discovered is that the kind of detailed biographical information that a person of interest has chosen to exclude from other, briefer bios is often included in a LinkedIn bio. Where usage of LinkedIn bio information becomes critical is in situations in which individuals falsely promote themselves as having degrees or other experience that turns out to be fraudulent. One such case involves the fabricated professional history of former New York charter school operator, Ted J. Morris, Jr.

On November 24, 2014, I wrote a blog post about Ted Morris, Jr.'s credentialing fraud.[35]

Ted Morris, Jr. seemed too good to be true, in part because he reported holding advanced degrees at only 22 years old. A news article celebrating Morris quickly led to questions about Morris's credentials, including a school administrator attesting that Morris did not receive a high school diploma from the school he said he had, as well as fellow blogger Peter Greene's calculations that Morris first applied to open a charter school when he was only 18 years old.

A LinkedIn search of Ted Morris was called for. However, the name, "Ted Morris," is pretty general, and I wanted to be certain to find the correct Ted Morris. So, using the information I had about Morris applying to open a charter school, I conducted a Google search about applicants named Ted Morris who wanted to open a charter school in New York, and by reading the actual charter school application, I discovered

Morris's more descriptive name, Ted J. Morris, Jr.

Once I knew Morris's more detailed name, I was ready to conduct a LinkedIn search. The way in which I conduct many of my LinkedIn searches is by simply typing the name of the person of interest and adding "LinkedIn" to a Google keyword search. In this case, I used "ted j morris jr linkedin" as my search term, and I discovered a rather lengthy LinkedIn bio on Morris, which was laden with false information, including his supposedly receiving a master's degree from a school that did not offer such a master's degree, as well as an alleged doctoral dissertation that did not exist.

A word of advice is needed for those using documents on professional online sites or social media to reveal unpleasant truths about individuals of investigatory interest. Assume that as soon as the undesired information is publicized, social media/professional online site information used as supporting evidence will disappear from public view, either by being deleted/altered or by becoming password protected. Thus, it may prove useful to take a snapshot of the information in question to preserve the record. Such proved true in the case of Ted Morris's LinkedIn bio, which was deleted within hours of my publishing my November 2014 post on Morris. In that case, a reader had the foresight to photograph Morris's LinkedIn bio and send it to me, and I added the photographed LinkedIn record to my posting.

SOCIAL MEDIA AND BLOGS

Our LinkedIn discussion leads us to another excellent source of information when researching individuals. Social media, including but not limited to Facebook, Twitter, and personal online platforms such as blogs can be used to discover a person's opinions, involvements, and history, including personal relationships, all of which can be useful in providing leads for additional research or ends in themselves depending upon the goals of a given research pursuit.

One way in which I have used social media/blogs to investigate relationships related to potential conflicts of interest concerned the questions surrounding the marriage status of the Louisiana state superintendent, John White. As a public official, White is supposed to include his wife and her employment information on his public ethics disclosure forms (for more on ethics disclosure filings, see the discussion of campaign finance filings later). In July 2017, I found that he had stopped doing so in 2013 despite the fact that his wife blogged three years later, in 2016, about still being married to White.[36] The story became more complicated as my research uncovered two social scene news articles, one a reprint of the other, dated October 2015 and November 2015, respectively. However, in the initial printing, John White's name was altered to read "Max White," presumably to disguise his attending the event with former Louisiana Department of Education (LDOE) employee, Katherine Westerhold. According to Westerhold's LinkedIn bio, she left LDOE to become director of policy for an organization that LDOE does business with, Relay Graduate School of Education.

The only other place that I could find information about Westerhold was her Facebook page, which happened to feature what appeared to be wedding pictures where the groom was John White. (For details, see my July 12, 2017, posting.[37]) White's role as state superintendent and his second wife's role as a director of an organization with which White does business posed ethical concerns, and I was able to bring the situation to public attention by using the information from Facebook in my July 2017 posting. In August 2017, White formally sought advice from the Louisiana board of ethics, an action which I blogged about in December 2017.[38]

"PDF" AS PART OF KEYWORD

Although I have found LinkedIn to be an excellent source for bio info on individuals involved in ed reform, I have also encountered instances in which individuals have either removed or chosen to exclude past experience from their LinkedIn bios or have deleted the entire LinkedIn bio altogether, which raises the question of why a person would try to conceal or erase past professional experience.

One such situation involved the former LDOE assistant superintendent, Rebecca Kockler, who left Louisiana for the position of chief of staff with the Los Angeles Unified School District (LAUSD). At the time that I first wrote about Kockler in March 2013,[39] she had a LinkedIn bio, and her extensive past experience with TFA, including experience as a TFA New York vice president, made for a significant part of Kockler's professional experience. However, by the time I wrote about her new job with LAUSD in June 2018,[40] not only had Kockler's LinkedIn bio disappeared, but it also appeared that she had scrubbed her other online bios of her TFA experience. Given that Kockler had risen in the TFA New York ranks to the position of a vice president, it simply had not occurred to me that a person on a rising career path in ed reform would ever want to conceal such information, so I did not think of preserving Kockler's LinkedIn bio as a screen shot.

In cases in which I am seeking archived information that is not readily available in Google searches, I include the term, "pdf" in my keyword search. Inclusion of "pdf" produces exactly that—PDF documents, including applications, meeting agendas, minutes, and presentation materials, formal review documents, resumes and curricular vitae predating the advent of the internet, and research papers. I first discovered the potential research treasure yielded by including "pdf" as part of a Google keyword search when I was writing my book, *Common Core Dilemma: Who Owns*

Our Schools?,[41] and was able to access the November 14, 2007, Illinois State Board of Education minutes,[42] which offered a rare glimpse into the messaging surrounding the Common Core State Standards.

In seeking complete professional information on Kockler, the Google search, "rebecca kockler bio pdf" yielded a 296-page, 2016 LDOE federal grant application, page 65 of which is Kockler's bio, including all of her TFA experience.[43]

One final word about PDF documents. There may be times in which the PDF cannot be copied and pasted because the PDF itself is a picture or series of pictures, as is the case when one views a document using the limited, free-access version of Adobe Acrobat. In such instances, I realized that I can sometimes copy and paste such documents using "print preview." Moreover, in some cases, the document must be copied in "blocks," because the text itself can only be copied as photos of blocks of text, and then reassembled in the same order via pasting. Even though this technique might allow one to skirt paying fees for permission to copy a document owned by another agency, I have not used this technique to avoid paying for permission to reproduce documents, and I am not advocating that readers commit academic theft by doing so, either. That noted, documents that belong in the public domain, such as state and federal grant applications for taxpayer funding, do not belong to any private entity and, as such, may be freely reproduced.

NEWSPAPER ARCHIVES

There are research queries in which one must go so far back in time that the pdf-keyword search is not practical. In these cases, accessing newspaper archives may prove a better option for researching individuals of public interest. Here I detail two situations in which I have found newspaper archives particularly useful. The first involves researching the US Department of Education (USDOE) Secretary of Education and zealous, billionaire school choice advocate, Betsy DeVos, specifically as concerns her mother's background as a public school teacher. The second concerns late United Federation of Teachers (UFT) president Al Shanker's emerging concerns about the potential exploitation of the charter school concept that he initially supported.

US Secretary of Education Betsy DeVos has an established history of actively promoting school choice, including charter schools, but also of favoring vouchers.[44] DeVos has zero experience as a classroom teacher, and her ideology is anti-traditional public school. However, in her USDOE bio, DeVos advertises that her "interest in education was sparked at an early age by her mother, a public school teacher."[45]

In an effort to discern the degree of truth in DeVos' statement about her mother, I accessed Michigan's newspaper archives from the 1950s. Through news articles about DeVos' mother, born Elsa Zwiep, I was able to glean enough information to verify that Zwiep taught public school for a few years, and that by the time young Betsy would have been able to remember it, was no longer a public school teacher.[46]

It is important to note that combing through newspaper archives can be a tedious business and may well entail piecing together the details of a story of interest. In the case of Zwiep's teaching history and its limited overlap with DeVos' childhood, I used information from three archived articles—the public notice of Zwiep's 1954 mid-year hire, her 1953 wedding announcement, and a 2013 article honoring Zwiep—as well as public info stating that DeVos was born in 1958.

However, an important lesson about the value of archives rests in the kind of articles that proved useful in this case. One was a job announcement, and another was a marriage announcement. Indeed, over the course of my years of researching individuals involved with ed reform, I have found marriage, divorce, and death announcements useful in both establishing personal relationship connections among reformers and in identifying alternative names in order to be certain that I could accurately identify the individual I was researching. In the case of women, this might be a surname prior to marriage or following a divorce or remarriage. In the case of men, it might be a middle name, middle initial, or suffix to add detail to a popular first- and last-name pairing. In order to verify a name or to discover/verify familial connections, I often Google the name with which I am familiar and include the keywords, "wedding," "marriage," "obituary," or "divorce."

As for online news archive search engines, I have used two that require a subscription but which also offer a free trial period—Newspapers. com, and Newspaperarchive.com—and using these two, I was able to complete my research within the period of the free trial. Both sites offer access to a number of papers nationwide, both have keyword search capabilities, and both allow downloading PDF copies of articles.

I have also accessed for free the archives of the *Chicago Tribune* when I was writing about the history of education reform in Chicago for my first book, *A Chronicle f Echoes: Who's Who in the Implosion of American Public Education.*[47]

Finally, when I was writing about the history of charter schools in my book, *School Choice: The End of Public Education?*, I accessed *The New York Times* "Where We Stand" news column archives of the former United Federation of Teachers (UFT) president, the late Al Shanker, for free via the New York State United Teachers (NYSUT) website.[48]

Of course, these archive sources are not exhaustive, and one may easily discover others by Googling a name with the term "news archives." For example, a 2019 Google search of "arne duncan news archives" produced a USDOE archive of speeches given by Duncan, as well as his successor John King.[49]

INTERNET ARCHIVES: THE WAYBACK MACHINE AND GOOGLE CACHE

On the topic of archives, allow me to note that one can also access archives of web pages via the internet archive search engine starting with my preferred engine, the Wayback Machine,[50] and ending with a word about Google Cache.[51]

As of this writing The Wayback Machine is accessible free of charge. However, one can also subscribe to the site, and one can donate to the site. The site is easy to use. If a link has gone dead, is otherwise inaccessible, or if one simply wants to view the link as it appeared at a particular time in the past, one can type the original link in the Wayback Machine search engine and hit "search." The results could span anywhere from hours to decades of periodic screen shots taken of a site. There is no guarantee of any certain number of screen shots within a given time frame. There might be multiple shots taken on a single day, or only one shot taken in a given calendar year, or no shots taken across multiple years.

By copying the archived link for a particular screen shot, one can access that shot at any time. For example, for my May 19, 2019, post on Center for Education Reform (CER) founder Jeanne Allen,[52] I wanted to see how the manner in which she represented herself in her CER bio sketch changed over 20+ years. So, I put the link for Allen's bio into the Wayback Machine, and I was able to view many of her bio sketches from 1996 to 2019, except for 2018 for which no screen shots were available. However, the link to Allen's bio sketch also changed across decades. In order to locate older versions of the link, I searched for archives of the CER home page and I was able to click on older versions of Allen's bio sketch links and access archived screen shots of those.

Note that the Wayback Machine may not offer access to links that cannot be "crawled,"[53] such as those for LinkedIn bios. Even so, the Wayback Machine is able to access social media such as Twitter, and unlike Google's "cache" feature, which is often available as an option when one right-clicks on a link that is the result of a Google search, the Wayback Machine offers the possibility of viewing multiple archived screen shots. In the case of Google Cache, if Google offers a cached option for the link, it is a single view and will be replaced by a subsequent screen shot whenever Google decides to update the cached link. Nevertheless, I find Google Cache useful for quick access to articles when the original link does not work.

THE PUBLISHED INTERVIEW

One of the more fruitful venues for obtaining firsthand information that might otherwise prove difficult to procure because of its obscurity is the interview. Online publications often interview individuals of interest to researchers and offer transcripts of those interviews, in whole or in part, as part of a featured article. Sometimes an article includes the entire interview in video or audio format. Although it might be tedious to transcribe the interview, depending upon the research purpose, it might be worthwhile to do so, if for no other reason than to present key portions of an interview in their full context.

That said, one should be careful not to violate any copyright, and this is especially a concern if one is making a profit from the transcribed interview or is somehow affecting the profitability of the publication originally posting the interview. In such cases, one should contact the publisher of the original interview for guidance and written permissions related to offering a transcribed copy of a heretofore untranscribed interview.

Videoed interviews may be publicly cross-posted to YouTube, with the publishing entity choosing to enable "embedding" the video in other venues. In these cases, since the publisher has already elected to make the interview content both available to the public and transportable for posting elsewhere, there is no problem transcribing the interview content and offering it to the public while being sure to credit and link to the original source.

Two situations in which publicly-available interviews of key persons have proven useful in my research involve the fate of a New Orleans high school and the thoughts of a noted econo-

mist on compulsory education. In both cases, the
telling information proved to be a brief section of
a longer interview.

In the first case, in 2012, Los Angeles-based
ed reformer Steve Barr, then of Green Dot charter
schools, was given control of New Orleans-based
John McDonogh Senior High School, which he
was supposed to renovate. After two years had
passed, in 2014 the school building still sat in its
decaying state, no work had been done on the
school, and Barr bailed on the project, but not
until Oprah Winfrey had been granted access
to the school to feature it in a series, *Blackboard
Wars*.[54] After Winfrey and Barr were both done,
New Orleans Recovery School District (RSD)
superintendent Patrick Dobard tried to portray
the situation as "a fresh start."[55]

I did not want the public to forget that it had
heard once before of McDonogh's so-called "fresh
start" in early 2012, when it was portrayed as such
by John White, who had just been promoted to
state superintendent after having arrived from
New York only five months earlier, in May 2011,
to become New Orleans RSD superintendent.[56]

By Googling "john white john mcdonogh," I
was able to find White's directly-stated, Steve Barr
renovation fanfare pitch as part of his February
2012 *Straight Up* interview with Rick Hess:

> RH: Post-Katrina, there were concerns
> about outsiders invading New Orleans
> schooling. There have been intense racial
> politics. How did you negotiate that during

your time at the RSD, and how does that shape your approach going forward?

JW: It's extremely important as a leader to never give up on your ideals. But on the other hand, never give up on respecting everyone at the table. That gives you a baseline of credibility off of which to operate.

RH: Can you offer an example of how you do this?

JW: Yes, at John McDonogh High School. When I first came to New Orleans, the word on the Street was we were going to shut down the building of that 100-year-old high school. And now we've announced that we are spending $35 million to renovate it. Steve Barr [founder of Green Dot Public Schools] and teachers now are going to take over the school's management...By staying at the table, by sitting through the discussion, by always insisting that this can be a college and career school, we had a compelling vision that attracted great partners, and are in a position to turn one of the lowest performing high schools in the country into a real beacon for change.[57]

By 2014, the "great partners" bailed on a project that they allowed to wallow in its own decay for two years, a decay that they did not have to drive past every day. The building remained a community eyesore for four more years. Steve Barr suffered no consequences, and John White gave no more glowing interviews about McDonogh's future. In 2018, the McDonogh Senior High school building was finally renovated, and a charter school, Bricolage Academy, moved in.[58]

The second situation in which a published interview proved useful in capturing the mindset of a noted market-minded ed reform name involved the January 1995 interview on Reason. com with the "father of school choice," Milton Friedman. In writing my book, *School Choice: The End of Public Education?*[59] I believed that a purely market-based system of school choice could not be reconciled with the concept of compulsory education. That is, if there are laws requiring children to be educated, then there must be some mechanism in place to be sure that such education happens—for example, other schools would be required to enroll students whose "first choice" school was at capacity. If a store sells out of a product, so far as the store is concerned, the consumer is out of luck. The store has no obligation to make sure the consumer is able to purchase the product elsewhere. Not so with compulsory education. If a chosen school cannot enroll a student, and if there is no oversight to be certain that all children are enrolled in some school, then that student could well end up with either piecemeal school attendance or, for lack of oversight, none at all.

In writing about economist and "father of

school choice" Milton Friedman's positions on school choice, I needed to find some clear discussion of his thoughts on compulsory education. I did not think he would be in favor of government-mandated education, which means he would be in favor of risking having some students "fall through the cracks" of a system that by design would benefit some but would not guarantee an education "product" for all.

In Friedman's 1995 interview with Reason. com, he discussed his thoughts on compulsory education, and in that discussion, it was evident that he was willing to set a pretty low bar in order to dispense with compulsory education. Whereas Friedman admitted vacillating on the idea of compulsory education, in the end, he leaned toward favoring school choice in the form of school vouchers at the possible expense of guaranteeing an education for all children. From the interview:

> If in the absence of compulsory education, only 50 percent would be literate, then I can regard it as appropriate.

> Some issues are open and shut. ... But education is not open and shut. In *Capitalism and Freedom* we came out on the side of favoring compulsory schooling and in *Free to Choose* we came out against it. ... I see the voucher as a step in moving away from a government system to a private system. Now maybe I'm wrong, maybe

it wouldn't have that effect, but that's the reason I favor it.[60]

As I point out in chapter 4 of *School Choice: The End of Public Education?*,[61] in 1996, the year after the above interview, Friedman and his wife Rosa started the Friedman Foundation expressly to advance market-based, school choice.

THE PERSONAL INTERVIEW

In October 2015, Alabama's 2014-15 Teacher of the Year, Ann Marie Corgill, abruptly resigned. On October 31, 2015, I wrote about Corgill's resignation.[62] Below is the issue, in sum:

> Corgill began the 2015-16 school year teaching second grade but was moved to fifth grade.
>
> The state says that she now needs to renew her state certification to include teaching fifth grade.
>
> But here's the kicker:
>
> When she was chosen as state teacher of the year, Corgill was teaching fourth grade— outside of her state certification.

On October 29, 2015, Corgill decided she had had enough and tended her resignation.

The news reports on Corgill's resignation were brief, and I was interested in learning the backstory. Corgill is not a promoter of corporate ed reform. Whereas most of my education research and writing focuses on individuals, organizations, and situations related to imposing market principals onto the public school classroom, I believed that Corgill probably had an riveting story to tell, and I was curious enough to hear it that I sought contact with her in order to request an interview. My ultimate goal in interviewing Corgill was to offer the transcribed interview to the public in order to shed light on the details of the situation and thereby inform the public. As such, the personal interview serves as a valuable, practical option.

In this instance, I was able to make initial contact with Corgill via Facebook. I sent her a friend request, and she accepted. It is important to know that in my Facebook profile, I identify myself as a Louisiana teacher, so even though Corgill did not know me personally, she could see that she and I share a profession. I would not have expected Corgill to accept my friend request if my Facebook profile were set up in such a way as to conceal my professional identity.

Once Corgill and I were Facebook friends, I was able to send her a personal message offering more information about who I was, my request for an interview, and my reason for the request— which was that I wanted to write about the details of her situation so that the public might hear her story in more detail. I was also willing to drive to Alabama to conduct the interview in person.

Had my ability to travel not been an option, we could have done an interview via email. Even so, it seemed both more personal and efficient to conduct a lengthy interview face-to-face, and to make arrangements as convenient as possible for Corgill.

Therefore, in November 2015, I took a personal day from school and drove the five hours to Birmingham, Alabama, in order to interview Corgill for several hours. I audio-taped the event, transcribed it, and posted it from November 2015 to January 2016 as a six-part series in which I offered Corgill the opportunity to "have the last word" by responding in a letter of reflection on the entire series.[63] The series is very informative and covers numerous topics, including state and local certification confusion, an unexpected school-level teacher shortage, and inadequate teacher compensation, all of which resulted in Corgill's once having to leave a beloved teaching job in New York because she could not afford the cost of living.

In interviewing Corgill, I kept my questions and comments brief in order to allow her to tell her story. I entered the interview with several guiding questions and consulted these as our interview progressed, but I mostly used what Corgill offered on a particular topic to inform subsequent questions. I often asked her to clarify comments she had made so that I, and by extension my readers, would clearly understand her narrative. Though I occasionally commented about my own professional experience, I purposely allowed her to do most of the talking. After all, that was the point of my visit.

A second, important personal interview that I conducted was in January 2016, and it was very much connected to my principal research focus of ed reform issues, namely, the post-Katrina, market-based ed reform domination of the New Orleans system of public schools. The individual I interviewed was New Orleans parent activist, Ashana Bigard. Bigard and I met in a New Orleans coffee shop on January 18, 2016, so that I might interview her about insider knowledge of the impact of the education reform presence in New Orleans. Our discussion included the closing of traditional public schools, the opening of charter schools in their place, and the impact that change has had on the community. The result was a 27-page interview, which I transcribed in full and offered to the public as a research resource preserved and indefinitely available for public access.[64]

Some final words about conducting personal interviews. Regarding transcribing, I prefer to transcribe the "slow and tedious" way of listening to an audio (or a video, as the case may be) a few words at a time, typing these, then returning to the recording to repeat the process until I am finished. Yes, there are transcription software programs available, and some interviews online offer written transcripts produced by automated means. Nevertheless, when it is important for me to quote someone exactly—including communication nuances—I prefer not to rely upon automated transcription because it is possible for the automated transcription to incorrectly transcribe words.

Furthermore, in the absence of important characteristics of conversation, including voice inflection, tone, and speaking speed, I find it almost always more important to capture as much in the transcript via effective usage of grammar and punctuation. I have found that even when automated transcription uses grammar and punctuation, such usage is rudimentary compared to what might be employed as the result of transcription by the human ear. The exception is in my using automated transcripts of business meetings, where capturing the emotion of the speaker is usually not a critical issue.

Next, one might note that the two personal interviews I offer as examples were with individuals who were not promoting ed reform, which means that we were on the same, locally-elected-board-operated side of traditional public education. As one might expect, it is easier to interview a person who holds the same ideological position as the interviewer. That acknowledged, there are times as an interviewer when I ask "devil's advocate" questions in order to hear a person's arguments in response to opposing positions and solutions.

Of course, it is possible for one to interview a person on the opposite side of an issue. In establishing contact and arranging such an interview, one must be particularly careful to engage in professional, civil discourse and certainly not attack the person regardless of dislike for or disagreement with a position. In the interview, ask pertinent, pointed questions, and let the interviewee's responses to those pointed questions tell the story. My favorite example of this concerns the 2017 Stone Lantern film, *Backpack Full of Cash*. In her interview for the film, Center for Education Reform founder and CEO Jeanne Allen inadvertently provided the film's final title when she responded as follows to an interview question about school choice:

> Our children have a backpack full of cash, and the school should vie for the privilege of having that backpack turned over to them.

Those words, which were used to title the film, are included as part of the trailer.[65] As one might expect when an individual's words are used to title a film that exposes problems associated with the very agenda that person promotes, Allen objected, saying in an October 5, 2017, article in *The Boston Globe* that her words had been taken out of context. On October 6, 2017, the film's producers responded to members on its mailing list (of which I am one) as follows:

> We stand by our reporting and believe Ms. Allen's words are used in their proper context in BACKPACK. We regret that

she doesn't like her portrayal in a film
that she hasn't seen, but also appreciate
that she's kept the conversation going on
the national level about the health of our
public school system.[66]

On October 08, 2017, I blogged about the
issue.[67] Both Allen and I happened to be in the
film, and I discussed the release form I signed
at the time of my interview in March 2014. The
form disclosed that interview material might be
used extensively, slightly, or not at all, and that
it was the producers' call. I also invited Allen
to publicize the entire conversation in order to
provide the context she believed the film omitted.
I even offered to publish her defense unedited. On
October 10, 2017, on LinkedIn, Allen published
another response in which she noted her dissat-
isfaction. In that response, she did not mention
the release that she, and I, and other interviewees
signed.[68]

Here is some potentially useful advice. If your
intention is to use personal interview content in a
professional manner, especially in a manner that
could earn a profit, seek legal advice regarding
the use of a formal written release of the interview
content, including details of whether the interviewee is waiving rights to compensation in rela-
tion to the interview. Even though I did not ask
Corgill or Bigard to sign releases for the content
of my interviews with them, if I were to use their
interviews as part of a book or other publication
for which I planned to be compensated, I would

expect my publisher to have me obtain signed release forms in order for me to use that interview content in the publication. Indeed, in the past, I had one publisher even require a signed release for emails that I had directly quoted in the book. Once the release is signed, the content of the emails now "belongs to" the book, and if I quote those emails again (as I have done in this book), I am quoting the previous book in which the email exchanges are now incorporated.

ARCHIVED SPEECHES

In this section on researching individuals, one last means of obtaining firsthand details concerning an individual's thoughts, expectations, goals, and positions is by accessing archived speeches for that individual. These archives usually take one of two forms, either written copies of the speech, or videoed presentations of the speaker giving the speech at an event such as a professional meeting, a celebration, or a community meeting. For high-profile individuals such as the Secretary of Education (both past and present), the US Department of Education (USDOE) offers speech archives.[69] Also, wealthy individuals who operate foundations, such as billionaire Bill Gates, may also provide links to archived speeches.[70]

It is usually easy to locate speeches of publicly-visible individuals by simply Googling the individual's name with the term "speeches." The tricky part is remembering that this is really only an option if one is investigating a high-profile individual. For example, Walmart heiress Alice Walton spent hundreds of millions of dollars trying to get the charter school cap lifted in Massachusetts in 2016. In my investigation of political action committee (PAC) donors to the 2016 Massachusetts "Yes on 2" campaign, I discovered that Arkansas-based Alice Walton was a major donor.[71] Since my focus was on the money flowing into Massachusetts from wealthy individuals in other states, my chief investigatory source was campaign finance reports (more to come on this in the section on investigating organizations). However, once I discovered Alice Walton's actions in pouring multiple millions of dollars into charter school promotion in another state, I could have turned my attention to her motivation for doing so. In such a case, my next step would have been to Google "alice walton speeches," which would have produced at least three videoed speeches by Alice Walton.

But let us step away from hypotheticals. In my discussion about the usefulness of obtaining public officials' emails via public records request, I noted that since officials often do not consider that their emails might be made public, they tend to divulge their true motivations and goals in their emails without glossing over issues that would raise eyebrows if publicly revealed. Even though the formal speeches of those who promote ed reform are meant for public consumption, the hypocrisy of the argument that market-based solutions are appropriate for some students but not for others can and does show itself in the speeches of ed reform promoters, if for no other reason than the audience might be comprised of those who will not be affected by the reforms. In other words, there is no need to be careful in shaping one's words to sell the ed reform message if the audience is not likely to be impacted by any distressing ed reform outcomes.

Consider, for example, Bill Gates's 2007 speech to Harvard's graduating class.[72] At the time, the Common Core State Standards (CCSS) were in the works, with key CCSS supporters approaching Gates to fund CCSS just one year later, in 2008.[73]

Digest that for a moment. A single billionaire was the driving force behind an education initiative intended to be expanded nationwide state by state. On August 27, 2013, I wrote a post in which I audited Gates' CCSS spending. It was the first in a five-part series.[74] Gates' CCSS funding continued for years, and in 2016 he was paying to connect CCSS with the USDOE's Every Student Succeeds Act (ESSA).[75] Thus, it is safe to conclude that Gates is fine with imposing his ideas about public education onto the USDOE.

Gates's hypocrisy reveals itself in his words about his time at Harvard, a university from which he dropped out. In my May 13, 2014, post, I confronted this hypocrisy as I compared Gates's purchase of his preferred education reform agenda, which includes CCSS but extends beyond it, with portions of his 2007 Harvard commencement speech. Here is an excerpt:

> In [a] four-minute, segment of his 2007 Harvard commencement speech, Gates notes learning about "education inequity." Of course, the irony lost on Gates is that if one comes from privilege like he does (he is speaking at Harvard, plus the high school Gates attended, Lakeside in Seattle, Washington, currently charges $28k per year tuition), one need not ever worry about some billionaire attempting to use him or her as an experiment in "common standards."

> Gates speaks about "taking on [education] inequities"..."in this age of accelerating technology":

>> ...in this age of accelerating technology, we can finally take on these inequities, and we can solve them.

> Gates talks about saving lives of children in other countries via delivery of medicine. He registers his surprise at discovering that "some lives" are deemed "worth saving, and others are not."

> Allow me to slightly alter Gates' words to suit his push of CCSS "implementation" onto a public education system from which he himself was exempt:

Some lives are "worth" the educational experiment that is CCSS, and others (those of the privileged) are not.

With Gates, it always seems to come back to "the market." He notes that "the market did not reward saving the lives of these children."

He notes that a problem with providing necessary medical assistance abroad is that the parents of these children "had no power in the market and no voice in the system."

Note what Gates is advocating: "Power in the market" translates into "voice in the system."

Yet Gates now wishes to unleash the CCSS experiment onto American public education because "scale is good for free market competition."[76]

It should be noted that between 1996 and 2018, Gates donated over $300M to Harvard University, so his being asked to speak at a Harvard commencement should come as no surprise. What is problematic is Gates's access to elected officials. When these organizations offer Gates the microphone at a formal meeting, they are giving him a powerful opportunity to promote his agenda in person. Such was the case of Gates's July 2009 address to the National Conference of State

Legislatures (NCSL).[77] Whereas in 2009 Gates had not yet directly funded the organization, he was given the position of "co-chair," and between 2013 and 2016, Gates paid NCSL $1.8M.[78] Gates is not a legislator, yet he was "co-chairing" a national legislative organization. The Gates Foundation has spent millions on its agenda in states nationwide, so there was leverage, and arguably there was also the hope that Gates money for NCSL would be forthcoming, which it duly was. Note also that "co-chair" Gates' 2009 speech came one year after he agreed to bankroll CCSS.[79]

In this speech, Gates was more than willing to tell his audience of state legislators what he believed they should do. Some excerpts:

> I hope you decide to accelerate reform....

> The institutions and innovations that are getting great outcomes should be expanded. Those that aren't should be changed or ended.

> To do this, we need to measure what matters. ...

> Without measurement, there is no pressure for improvement. ...

> I would urge the legislators here [with colleges] to start the push to greater measurement by asking the colleges and universities in your districts to publish their graduation rates....

Caps should be lifted for charter school operators who have a proven record of success.... We can make dramatic advances by replacing the worst schools with high-performing charters—operated by organizations with a great track record. ...

We need to take two enabling steps: we need longitudinal data systems that track student performance and are linked to the teacher; and we need fewer, clearer, higher standards that are common from state to state. The standards will tell the teachers what their students are supposed to learn, and the data will tell them whether they're learning it. ...

Fortunately, the state-led Common Core State Standards Initiative is developing clear, rigorous common standards that match the best in the world. Last month, 46 Governors and Chief State School Officers made a public commitment to embrace these common standards.

This is encouraging—but identifying common standards is not enough. We'll know we've succeeded when the curriculum and the tests are aligned to these standards.[80]

Remember that Gates had already committed in 2008 to fund a CCSS that was not yet written. Part of Gates's funding was for the National Governors Association and the Council of Chief State School Officers, the ones that made a "public commitment" to be state-led. Or rather, Gates-led. And Gates used his 2009 National Council of State Legislatures, "co-chair" speaking opportunity to prod those various legislators into joining his "state-led" CCSS cause.

Gates makes clear in this speech what he stands for—CCSS, lifting charter school caps, and grading teachers using student test scores. This makes the contents of this speech important for public awareness about how billionaires like Gates leverage their wealth to drive education policy.

RESEARCHING ORGANIZATIONS

In this section, I shift my attention to researching organizations. However, as I mentioned previously, organizations are comprised of individuals, so that investigating an organization often involves discovering information on the individuals either leading the organization, or benefiting from it, or both. Therefore, in this section on investigating organizations, readers should expect overlap with investigating individuals. Often when I begin investigating an individual associated with corporate-styled ed reform, I start by investigating the organizations to which that individual belongs, or from which the individual or the organizations benefit financially.

Since I ended the previous section with a discussion about billionaire funding and specifically Alice Walton and Bill Gates, it provides a useful segue to begin our focus on investigating organizations with a convenient means to do so provided by both the Bill and Melinda Gates Foundation and the Walton Family Foundation—

the foundation grants search engine.

NONPROFIT-GRANT SEARCH ENGINES

For many years, the Gates Foundation has offered a publicly-available search engine for those wishing to view its spending in the form of grants to other organizations, including nonprofits and governmental entities.[81] Circa 2018, the Walton Family Foundation (WFF) also began offering public search of its grants via a grants database.[82] Not all foundations offer such a service. In reality, most don't. Even so, since Walton and Gates are arguably the biggest philanthropic funders of ed reform initiatives, the fact that these two do offer such easily-accessible search capabilities provides a real edge for those wishing to know if Gates or Walton are paying a local, state, or national organization for education initiatives, including how much, how often, and to what end. In the case of the specific purpose of a grant and its disbursement schedule, as of this writing, the Gates search engine is superior to WFF's.

What is important about using these search engines is to know that conducting a search using what appears to be the full name of an entity of interest might yield no results because a word is misspelled, or one uses "of" in a name in which "for" is the term, or words in the prospective entity name are out of order.

For example, the school choice nonprofit for which Betsy DeVos was chair prior to her becoming US Secretary of Education is named the American Federation *for* Children (AFC).[83] This is easy to incorrectly transpose as the "American Federation *of* Children." When it comes to searching contributions for AFC, mistyping the "for" in the organization name as "of" yields no results. So, one must be careful to have the exact, correct name when searching for entities using full organization names. If there is any doubt, one can use parts of names, for example "American Federation," and then scroll through the search results until one locates the entity one is seeking.

But do be careful not to incorrectly focus on an organization with a similar name, while keeping in mind that an organization may appear under two names because it has had a name change. In the case of AFC, it was originally called, "Advocates for School Choice"[84] and then became also known as "doing business as" Alliance for School Choice.[85] Since AFC is a business entity, it has a nine-digit employer identification number (EIN)[86] that remains constant across organizational name changes. (More to come on EINs.)

ANNUAL AND OTHER ORGANIZATIONAL REPORTS

Prior to the WFF offering a search engine for its grantmaking, one means I used for identifying organizations receiving WFF contributions was the organization's annual reports. These are easy enough to locate on a foundation's website or by Googling the name of the foundation (even a partial name will do) along with the term, "annual reports." Also, one can add a specific year, for example "broad foundation annual report 2012." Once one has downloaded the annual report, consulting the table of contents for a section on "grants" usually takes the reader to the section of the report in which grantees are listed. The downside of searching for grant recipients via annual reports is that the exact grant amount and purpose might not be included in the report. For such details, one might have to consult the organization's tax forms. (More to come on this also.)

Some organizations publish "strategic" reports, which can span a number of years and the purpose of which is to strategically plan courses of action for implementing identified organizational goals. One such organization that publishes its strategic plan is the Walton family's WFF, and one of the Waltons' priorities is the expansion of school choice. As noted in the WFF's strategic plan for 2016–2020, the Waltons noticed that in expanding "school choice" by supporting charter schools, they were running into the problem of being viewed as too "top-down" in their efforts. So, in top-down fashion, they set out to create grass roots support for their desired school choice expansion. I wrote about this arrogant irony in my October 29, 2016, post.[87] Some excerpts from this post:

> It seems that from 2016 to 2020, the Waltons plan to particularly expand their presence in New Orleans (and DC and Denver). They have a new plan for school choice, as noted in this October 2015 Grantmakers for Education report.[88] ...

> The Waltons view their "strategy" as somehow neutral. You know, "We fund all sorts of schools, without bias towards charters... But, oh, yeah, we really prefer charters, as our spending history clearly attests":

>> The Foundation sees its strategy as agnostic with regard to sector (public charter schools, traditional public schools, private schools). ... The Foundation's funding history includes a significant amount of support for charter schools, however. In fact, roughly two-thirds of the Education Program's investments support the growth of a high-quality charter sector in some way. This seeming preference for charter schools is in line with the Foundation's theory of change that requires change agents, like new, high-quality charter schools, to increase competition in citywide school systems....

> The Waltons do not see themselves as

buying up democracy in order to shape
it into the Image of Walton. And they
are concerned about building grass roots
support for their imposed reform. It seems
that they thought the grass roots support
would just happen and would manifest
itself in automatic "competition" between
charters and traditional public schools.
Such competition has not happened, so
the Waltons want to increase their funding
(and presence) in three key cities in order
to petri-dish their latest strategic plan,
which will now include grit and determination:

> The Walton Family Foundation's origi-
> nal theory of change was that expand-
> ing choice would spur competition,
> and consequently create system-
> wide improvements. The Founda-
> tion thought that once choice options
> reached a critical mass or sufficient
> "market share," transformational,
> system-wide change would begin to
> occur. With over 20 years of learning
> from grantees and their communities,
> the Foundation's theory of change is
> evolving and expanding. As Marc
> Holley describes it, "We have come
> to the realization that choice in and
> of itself is necessary but not suffi-
> cient to drive change at scale. We are
> more deliberate in thinking about

what needs to be in place in order to promote functioning choice." ...

From their perch at the top, the Waltons need to get the parents (the bottom) on their side:

One area where the Foundation has received criticism is in the area of community engagement. It has been accused of having a top-down approach that does not adequately address the needs and desires of parents, local advocacy groups, and community groups. This is an issue the Foundation is grappling with. "The provision of choice, and the publication of data on school performance, has sometimes had little impact, especially in districts where reform lacks adequate local ownership, community and wider civic involvement, and parent engagement," [Walton Foundation Senior Advisor] Bruno Manno notes. He identifies two levers in engaging local partners and communities more thoroughly: 1) building an active coalition of supporters, and 2) cultivating local advocacy partners. "We need a local and civic base of support for the work that's going on. The work we support requires a stable constituency to be advocates for schools over time. There is a political dimension as well, the community and families need to understand what options are available." ...[89]

What is particularly useful about reading the strategic reports of ed reform billionaire promoters like the Waltons is that one can learn of the future plans of these moneyed ed reformers and use the information to alert would-be affected communities. One can also gain a window into the thinking of such organizations and publicize their out-of-touch foolishness, in this case the Walton idea of purchasing grass roots support for billionaire-derived, billionaire-driven, ed reform goals.

In seeking to locate organizational strategic plans, one can consult the press releases of the organization. For example, by Googling "walton family foundation press releases," I was able to easily find the WFF newsroom link.[90] One can also Google the name of an organization with terms such as "strategic plan," "grant making goals," or more specifically "education plan." Googling "walton family foundation strategic plan" brought me to the K12 education page for WFF, which includes a link to its strategic plan.[91]

WHO'S FUNDING WHOM?

Many practical research investigations focus on the spending and receiving of money. In the case of ed reform-promoting billionaires like Gates, Walton, and others like the Eli and Edythe Broad Foundation,[92] the research is logically centered on their spending, not their receiving. Billionaire and millionaire ed reform-friendly foundations are a principal money source for market-based education reform, other primary sources being tax dollars and businesses, such as hedge funders. Walton, Gates, and Broad are not receiving money to promote ed reform. They are doling it out. Thus, the focus of investigating education reform-promoting philanthropy is to discover the individuals and organizations receiving money from the uber-wealthy that is earmarked for education reform.

But let us first make a side-step to answer the question, "How can one tell whether a foundation is indeed promoting a certain agenda, in this case, one of corporate ed reform?"

The answer is to Google the organization's website and read about its positions and organizational goals related to a specific area, such as education.

For example, let's say that in my research, I come across the Max and Marjorie Fisher Foundation. I Google "fisher foundation," and I immediately see a link for their website.[93] There are links for "who we are," "impact areas," "special initiatives," and "grant partners." In reading these links, I see that the foundation's only educational focus is early education, not K12 education, and very few of its education grant recipients[94] are ed reform organizations. So I conclude that the Max and Marjorie Fisher Foundation is not a market-based ed reform force.

Let me offer a word of caution to the zealous. Be careful blackballing a foundation like the Max and Marjorie Fisher Foundation for funding a few questionable entities, such as known education reform organizations. The majority of the Max and Marjorie Fisher Foundation early childhood grants are to organizations not aligned with corporate ed reform. If there is any doubt on this front, simply review the websites of the grantees to determine whether the grantees promote ed reform.

What is important to note is that the Max and Marjorie Fisher Foundation has no sweeping corporate education reform agenda, and as previously noted, no K12 ed agenda at all. When a foundation supports education in general by paying grants to a number of education organizations, it is possible that one or two will be education reform organizations.

But what if the one or two ed reform organizations that the Max and Marjorie Fisher Foundation supports happen to also be major forces in the dismantling of K12 public education? In this case, I would be surprised if the foundation's goals did not include a market-based ed reform bent.

However, if the foundation does not appear to especially endorse corporate education reform but is still financing some major education reform organizations, one could always contact the foundation via a respectfully-worded email in which the writer is clearly identified, and in which information meant to enlighten the foundation's board should be politely but not forcefully offered. The foundation might appreciate having a more complete perspective about its grantees and might alter its funding decisions accordingly.

The reality is that comparatively few organizations provide much of the philanthropic funding behind ed reform, in contrast to the many organizations receiving the funding.

There are many ways to uncover which organizations are on the receiving end of the dollars that keep them in business. The simplest course of action is to check the organization's website. If an organization does receive philanthropic funding, often the site will include a link for funders or donors, or the site will mention its funders somewhere on its home page.

Another way to quickly locate such info is to Google the name of the organization along with the keyword, "funders" or "donors." Even so, the dollar amount might not be listed, and the list of donors might not be comprehensive.

Therefore, consulting annual reports might prove more helpful in identifying a comprehensive donor listing. Keep in mind that by definition annual reports cover a single year, so consulting numerous annual reports might be necessary to establish a donor history for the organization.

NONPROFIT TAX FORMS

If one's research query concerns not-for-profit organization finances, one means of identifying both nonprofit donors and recipients is through examining nonprofit organization tax forms. Nonprofits are required by law to make their tax filings (IRS Form 990s) available to the public.[95] For the purpose of investigating nonprofit organizations related to education reform, the 990 is most likely to be one of the following:

1. A 990-PF, that is a "private foundation,"
2. A 990-EO that is a 501(c)(3) "exempt organization" that does not have lobbying as its primary activity—the 990 may not have "EO" written after the 990, just "990," or
3. A 990-EO that is a 501(c)(4) in which lobbying on behalf of "social welfare" may the organization's primary activity.[96]

It should be noted that according to IRS regulations, 501(c)(3) nonprofits are not allowed to "intervene in political campaigns or conduct substantial lobbying activities."[97] Otherwise, the 501(c)(3) risks losing its tax exempt status.[98] The chief difference between the PF and EO organizations is that the PF must identify contributors who contribute $5,000 or more to the nonprofit in a given tax year, whereas the EO does not have to identify its contributors by name.[99]

ACCESSING THE TAX FORMS

Although one can obtain tax filings for a nonprofit by contacting either the nonprofit or the Internal Revenue Service (IRS), it is increasingly easy to immediately access nonprofit tax forms online. On their websites, many foundations offer links to their most recent tax forms. Furthermore, there are a number of nonprofit tax form search engines, some of which charge a fee, but some do not. When searching online for nonprofit tax filings, I often utilize one or more of the following:

1. The IRS's tax exempt organization search,"[100]
2. The Foundation Center's "990 finder,"[101]
3. ProPublica's "Nonprofit Explorer,"[102] or
4. Conservative Transparency's 990 search engine.[103]

I utilize each of the four depending on the goals I have in mind.

I use the IRS search if I am trying to locate tax information on an organization with a generic or otherwise unclear name, first to verify that the nonprofit exists, and then in some cases to discover exactly when the IRS granted the organization nonprofit status. The IRS lookup produces a copy of the organization's "determination letter," the actual IRS notification of the granting of nonprofit status to the organization. I also like the IRS search when I am trying to locate an obscure organization's employee identification number (EIN). The EIN is a unique, federal tax identification number assigned to businesses operating in the US. Once I know the EIN, I can then Google the number itself in order to locate other documents and information referencing the nonprofit in question.

The Foundation Center's "990 finder" is the easiest to use because it offers the least intimidating start page. It also tends to offer information for multiple tax years if the nonprofit has existed for at least several years.

However, my favorite search is ProPublica's "Nonprofit Explorer." I actually conduct most of my ProPublica searches using Google, where I combine the name of the nonprofit with the terms, "990 propublica" to see if ProPublica has a record of the tax history of the nonprofit in question. What I like so much about ProPublica is that it tends to provide the most tax years of any search engine, going back to 2001 or 2002 if the organization has existed that long. It is also easy for me to share the entire ProPublica result using a single link. Finally, I find that ProPublica often offers the most recent tax information of any of the four search engines, the IRS included. The downside is that ProPublica sometimes has no record of a nonprofit for which I am searching, in which case I usually use Foundation Center's "990 finder" as my next course of action for the search.

Also, ProPublica sometimes divides the tax form into its individual parts—the main 990 form and then all of the supplementary schedules—which means one must remember to utilize the drop-down menu to access all schedules associated with a specific tax form.

What I appreciate most about Conservative Transparency's 990 search engine is that for nonprofits that have been around for decades, it is the site most likely to have tax information as far back as the late 1990s. Also, when using the site to search individuals to see which nonprofits those individuals are affiliated with, I find that Conservative Transparency is the site most likely to produce obscure nonprofits. That noted, I have also found that the results of such a search may not be exhaustive. Thus I suggest utilizing multiple nonprofit search engines to ensure more comprehensive results.

There are other nonprofit search engines, such as Guidestar[104] and CitizenAudit.[105] Each of these sites once allowed some degree of free access to 990s, but as of this writing, both sites charge fees. Even so, when I Google an organization name and include the keyword "990," I still sometimes use Guidestar to identify the nonprofit's EIN, which as of this writing Guidestar still allows the public to view for free without signing up for an account. This ability to freely view basic info in Guidestar is especially useful when the name of a nonprofit is so general that its name produces hundreds of hits in other search engines, as happens for example when searching for the nonprofit Education Trust.

With a number of options for actually locating 990s, next comes the question of what information is most useful from the nonprofit tax forms. I realize that the very idea of consulting tax forms is daunting for many individuals, but it need not be. Yes, I could write a fairly lengthy tutorial on the information one can glean from a 990. However, my goal in writing this part of the book was to distill my knowledge into a manageable section about what information from the tax forms is most often of greatest investigative interest. To that end I will use the details from several nonprofit tax forms as guides to identify noteworthy information while trying not to overwhelm readers.

Nevertheless, since discussion of tax forms is by nature technical, readers may find it useful to have available the actual tax forms that I cite in the end notes while reading this section on nonprofit tax forms. Doing so may enable readers to better follow the discussion.

AMERICAN ENTERPRISE INSTITUTE

First of all, let us use the American Enterprise Institute's (AEI) 2017 Form 990 as an example.[106] Note that I am utilizing ProPublica, which means I need to be aware that I might have to access the drop-down menu in order to view all associated schedules pertaining to the AEI tax form. From reading the first page, I can see that AEI (EIN 53-0218495):

1. Is located in Washington, DC,
2. Files according to the fiscal year, in this case from 07/01/17 to 06/30/18,
3. Is a 501(c)(3), which means it is not a lobbying organization, and
4. Is not a 990-PF, which means I should not expect it to identify its donors by name.

AEI describes its mission as follows:

The American Enterprise Institute is a community of scholars and supporters committed to expanding liberty, increasing individual opportunity, and strengthening free enterprise. AEI pursues these ideals through independent thinking and the highest standards of research and exposition.

AEI is what is known as a "conservative think tank." Its people read, research, and comment on policy in areas in which they often have little to no hands-on experience, even as they are perceived as experts by the media because of their think-tank affiliation.

From the AEI 990 first page, I also see that AEI collected $57M in "contributions and grants" (line 8) in FY2017, down from $61M in 2016. Still, that's a lot of money. I also notice that for both FY2016 and FY2017, AEI's "revenue less expenses" (line 19) was in the black, which means the organization is not living above its means, so to speak. I can also see that AEI had a lot of cash in the bank at the end of FY2017, since it was sitting on $320M in "net assets" (line 22).

Moving on to page 2. This page offers information on AEI's top three spending priorities. It can include more, but if there are three spending priorities, it must include at least three. Each spending priority includes a description of the priority, the amount expended, and any revenue generated from the priority. AEI's largest spending priority in FY2017 was $12.8M for "economic policy studies." At the bottom of page 2 is the total that AEI spent on "program services" in FY2017, which was $38.1M.

Now, we skip to pages 7 and 8, which lists "officers, directors, trustees, key employees, highest compensated employees, and independent contractors." This section is of particular interest because it details who is leading the organization—its executives and other board members—as well as each one's time devoted to the organization and total compensation.

What I immediately notice is that AEI president Arthur Brooks was paid $2.2M total compensation in FY 2017 for working 40 hours/week, and executive vice president David Gerson was paid $1M total compensation, also for working 40 hours/week.

I can also see that both Brooks' and Gerson's compensation came from AEI and not, in full or in part, from a "related organization" operated by or otherwise connected with AEI. By viewing Schedule J, I see that $1.3M of Brooks' compensation was designated as a "bonus," and that eight officers and the five "highest compensated employees" (13 individuals total) cost AEI $6.1M in FY2017.[107] And here is an argument for reviewing multiple tax year forms for the same organization—both Brooks' and Gerson's profoundly high total FY2017 compensation actually doubled from FY2016.[108]

As for AEI's highest paid independent contractors, the top listed was Sea Island Acquisition LLC at $1.8M for "conference expenses." If I wanted to, I could investigate SEA Island Acquisition via LLC lookup (more to come on this) to see if the company was owned by an AEI board member or executive to discern if the board was doing business with its own members. Such investigations might prove more important if the nonprofit were dependent upon public funding, as are charter schools, and if there were concerns about self-dealing, nepotism, or other conflicts of interest. As it is, AEI collected no revenue in FY2017 from "government grants" (page 9, line 1e).

AEI's FY2017 Schedule L shows "transactions with interested persons," which concerns payments to individuals related to board members, for example. In the case of AEI, board member Dick Cheney's wife, Lynne, received compensation totaling $89,600 as "employee compensation and 403B contribution."[109]

Schedule M details noncash contributions. AEI indicates that in FY2017, it received stock valued at $1.6M as a contribution.[110]

On its FY2017 tax form, AEI includes no disbursement of grants to individuals or to other organizations, and it lists one related organization, a real estate company. However, AEI operates no other nonprofits (see Schedule R).[111]

One final word about Form 990 schedules. AEI filed a Schedule O, "Supplemental Information to Form 990 or 990-EZ."[112] This form allows the nonprofit to explain in narrative form information appearing elsewhere on its tax form. Now, reading Schedule O can be tedious, but it can provide useful information, such as the terms of separation for terminated board members or employees, as well as clarification of business agreements and services that for some reason require explanation—for example, relationships between board members and vendors, or the disbursement of a seemingly large sum of money.

Among the mostly banal narratives on Schedules O, I have encountered some eyebrow-raising information regarding departures of board members and familial relationships between board members and vendors. In AEI's case, the organization used Schedule O to justify its FY2017 compensation decisions, including paying Brooks $2.2M, by noting that AEI considers "compensation of other chief executives with similar experience." I have yet to see another conservative think tank CEO paid $2.2M, up from $1.1M in the previous year, which seems to indicate that the justifications included on Schedule O need not touch reality.

EDUCATION TRUST

Let us now take an example in which a nonprofit operates other nonprofits. The ed reform nonprofit Education Trust does this. My Google search for "education trust 990 propublica" produced no useful results, but my subsequent search for "education trust 990" provided a Guidestar hit, and I was able to extract Education Trust's EIN (52-1982223) from the Guidestar result. Next, by Googling "52-1982223," I found a Foundation Center hit for the exact "education trust" that I was seeking. In comparison, a simple search for "education trust" in the Foundation Center 990 Finder produced 1,232 results.

The purpose of this search was to determine if Education Trust controls other related nonprofit organizations. So, once I opened Education Trust's 2016 Form 990,[113] I hit CONTROL+F so that I could search the 990 for the keywords, "related organizations," which is the term as it is used on the 990s. I scrolled through the hits until I reached page 52 of the 990, "Identification of Related Tax-Exempt Organizations" (Schedule R).

And there on page 52 I saw that Education Trust is the "controlling entity" for three other nonprofits, all of which are 501(c)(3) "not lobbying nonprofits":

1. Education Delivery Institute (EIN 30-0041047),
2. EdInnovations, Inc. (EIN 27-3195260), and
3. Data Quality Campaign, Inc. (EIN 27-4566795).

The tax filings for these organizations should all have the other three nonprofits listed as "related organizations." The importance of such information is that the nonprofits could appear to the public to be operating as unrelated entities, especially if the nonprofit names are quite different, as they are for Education Trust. When I first read of Data Quality Campaign (DQC), I had no idea it was controlled by Education Trust and was, by extension, promoting an agenda "controlled" by Education Trust. As of this writing, the DQC "who we are" page does not disclose this relationship.[114]

SUCCESS ACADEMY CHARTER SCHOOLS AND THE SUCCESS FOUNDATION

In a third example, let us consider payment to a nonprofit's CEO not only by that nonprofit, but also by a "related organization." Such is the case for Eva Moskowitz, CEO of the New York-based Success Academy Charter Schools, Inc. (SA). According to SA's FY2015 Form 990 (EIN 20-5298861),[115] Moskowitz received $679K in total compensation, most of it ($455K) from a "related organization."

The only related organization listed is the Success Foundation, Inc. (EIN 46-1501902).[116] Indeed, in FY2015, Moskowitz did receive $455K from the Success Foundation—for working a mere 5 hours/week. According to the tax form, Moskowitz earned an additional $192K for 50 hours/week of work as the SA CEO. What is also strange about this situation is that the FY2015 total revenue of the Success Foundation was only $703K, and its total expenses, only $691K, which makes the Success Foundation appear to exist chiefly to pay Moskowitz. The Success Foundation board includes Moskowitz (the only compensated member), the two hedge funders whose idea it was to start Success Academy charter schools, Joel Greenblatt and John Petry (basically Moskowitz's bosses),[117] and another businessman, Chuck Strauch.[118]

Eva Moskowitz answers to the hedge funders whose brainchild charter schools she oversees, and by paying her two-thirds of her total compensation via a nonprofit that they essentially control, Greenblatt and Petry could severely cut her salary at will. They also sit on the SA board, but there are 17 other board directors, such that Greenblatt's and Petry's influence is not nearly as prominent. Perhaps that is why they formed the Success Foundation. I described the Greenblatt-Petry influence over Moskowitz's SA compensation in my April 27, 2018, blog post.[119]

RESULTS IN EDUCATION FOUNDATION

One notable situation illustrating the utility of nonprofit tax forms for discovering information on education reform organizations concerns the nonprofit Results in Education Foundation (RIEF, EIN 47-0988089).

On September 1, 2014, *The Washington Post* journalist Lyndsey Layton published an article introducing a new ed reform organization, Education Post. From Layton's article:

> Into the fray steps Education Post, a nonprofit group that plans to launch Tuesday with the aim of encouraging a more "respectful" and fact-based national discussion about the challenges of public education, and possible solutions.
>
> Peter Cunningham, the former communications guru for U.S. Education Secretary Arne Duncan, is leading the organization, which is backed with initial grants totaling $12 million from the Broad Foundation, Bloomberg Philanthropies, the Walton Family Foundation and an anonymous donor.[120]

As I noted in my April 21, 2016, post,[121] Layton identified Education Post as a "nonprofit." On its website, Education Post does so, as well, at the bottom of its "about" page:

We are a nonprofit, nonpartisan communications organization dedicated to building support for student-focused improvements in public education from preschool to high school graduation.[122]

Nowhere on the Education Post website does it indicate another name for its nonprofit. As of this writing, when I Google, "Education Post 990," the only hits I get related to the organization are my own work. So, in 2016 when I was investigating Education Post's "anonymous donor," I first had to investigate the name under which the nonprofit was registered.

To do so, I started with what I knew. In her 2014 article, Layton identified Broad, Bloomberg, and Walton as financial supporters of Education Post. So, I began perusing the 2014 990s of the Eli and Edythe Broad Foundation, Bloomberg Philanthropies, and the Walton Family Foundation (WFF). My goal was to work backwards—to read the grants sections of the tax forms of these three nonprofits in order to possibly discover the official name of the "nonprofit," Education Post.

Now, the tax forms can be extensive for billionaire-operated philanthropic nonprofits. The Broad Foundation has one of the shorter forms—its 2014 Form 990 is only 70 pages long. Fortunately, there is the option to conduct a keyword search using CONTROL +F. When I searched for "education post" in Broad's 2014 Form 990,[123] I found the explanation for a $1M grant to Results in Education Foundation, to "support startup of education post."

When I subsequently Googled "results in education foundation 990," I encountered problems associated with searching an arguably generic name. Adding "propublica" to my search produced no useful result. So, I turned to Foundation Center's 990 Finder and searched "results in education foundation," and there it was, Results in Education Foundation, RIEF (EIN 47-0988089).

What I also discovered was that RIEF is a 990-PF, which means it must identify those contributors who donated $5,000 or more to the nonprofit. And so it does, on page 2 of Schedule B (page 15 of the return). It turns out that the anonymous donor was Emerson Collective, a limited liability company (LLC) registered in California in 2011 to Steve Jobs' widow, Laurene Powell Jobs.[124] Powell Jobs' company donated $500,000.

Two mysteries solved. Even so, note that it takes time for nonprofit tax filings to be made public. In the case of RIEF, Layton announced Education Post in September 2014, the tax year ended December 2014, but RIEF's 2014 tax filing was not received by the IRS until November 25, 2015, and it took a few months for the filing to appear on the search engine I used at the time, CitizenAudit, which was in the winter of 2016. But it was definitely worth writing about because in concealing its true "Results in Education Foundation" name, the "nonprofit" Education Post was well poised to escape the scrutiny to which the public is entitled when it comes to organizations granted the privilege of paying no taxes. As of this writing, Education Post still does not identify itself by its actual nonprofit name, Results in Education Foundation.

As a final word for this section, allow me to mention that the IRS website offers numerous concise yet informative pages regarding charities and other nonprofits. I suggest it as a first stop for those wishing to advance their knowledge of nonprofit operations beyond the scope of my brief tutorial.[125]

CORPORATE FILINGS SEARCH

My efforts to locate information about Emerson Collective—the RIEF anonymous donor—bring us to the next tool available to those investigating ed reform, the corporate filings search. Corporations, LLCs (limited liability companies), partnerships, and nonprofits, all of which may be termed "corporations," are usually required to register their existence with some state agency, such as the secretary of state.[126] Many states now offer online search engines for a corporation's articles of incorporation and other filings, such as annual reports. Some states may provide summary information free of charge and then charge a fee for additional detailed filings, while other states provide links to PDF copies of actual filings free of charge.

Let me use Emerson Collective as an example.

From the RIEF tax form, I noted the address of Emerson Collective as being in California, so I knew that I was seeking information about a California organization. Had I not known, I could have Googled "emerson collective" and sought an address at the bottom of its web page or as part of its "contact us" information. However, as it so happens (at least at the time of this writing), the Emerson Collective website does not mention it is located in California.[127] The "about" page does identify Laurene Powell Jobs, but it does not identify Emerson Collective by corporation type.[128]

In order to search for corporate information on Emerson Collective, I needed to know in what state the corporation is registered. So, had I started my search with trying to discover the state in which Emerson Collective is located, I could have used ProPublica's nonprofit tax form "full text search"[129] and sought address information via the appearance of Emerson Collective on its nonprofit tax form. What I did learn from such a search is that "Emerson Collective" did not appear as the name of a nonprofit, and RIEF did not appear as one of the hits for the term, "emerson collective."

I could also have Googled, "emerson collective address," which would have immediately yielded a Bloomberg "snapshot" identifying Emerson Collective as an LLC located in Palo Alto, CA.[130]

Knowing that Emerson Collective is located in California allows me to then Google "california llc search" to locate the California Secretary of

State's "business search" page.[131] By then choosing "LP/LLC name" and searching "emerson collective," I am able to see a search result for two options, Emerson Collective, LLC (registration date 06/28/2011) and Emerson Collective Investments, LLC (registration date 06/27/2012).

Clicking on "Emerson Collective, LLC" brings me to "entity detail," which includes links to three PDF documents—the registration/articles of corporation (06/28/2011), and two single-page, periodic reports from 2015 and 2019. On these documents, Powell Jobs is listed as the "organizer" of Emerson Collective. Such information is particularly useful when organization leadership is unclear.

Sometimes it is more difficult to identify both the registered name of an organization and the state in which it is registered. The company might not even exist. A colleague asked me if I would locate information on "Educational Properties TCGIS [Twin Cities German Immersion School] LLC," which was connected to an Orleans Parish School Board (OPSB) member, Kathleen Padian, complete with a New Orleans residential address oddly listed on a 2013 Ramsey County, Minnesota, property tax bill for the school.[132] Padian is also a partner with Louisiana-based TenSquare, LLC, a charter school strategy company.[133]

As for Educational Properties TCGIS, LLC, corporate entity searches for both Louisiana and Minnesota produced no results. I also conducted a search in Delaware since Delaware is a preferred state for registering LLCs for a number of reasons, including the minimal startup information required and low annual fees.[134] No results. So, I set out on a Google search of "TCGIS history" and came up with a May 10, 2019, document that was signed by someone from the "Twin Cities German Immersion School Building Company,"[135] a nonprofit that is on file in Minnesota, effective 12/16/2014,[136] and that identifies itself as the owner of the school building in question. By using details from the TGCIS history result, I was able to discern that TenSquare LLC might have intended to create Educational Properties TCGIS LLC, but it never did. Twin Cities German Immersion School Building Company, a Minnesota nonprofit not connected to either Louisiana-based TenSquare or to Padian, owned the school in 2019.

CAMPAIGN FINANCE/ETHICS DISCLOSURES

Another means of obtaining public information involves accessing a state's campaign finance filings and ethics disclosures. In my section on social media, I offered an example in which I accessed Louisiana state education superintendent John White's ethics disclosures. In states that require public officials to file ethics disclosure statements, those filings can often be found by accessing the state's public records website or by Googling the state name with the keywords, "public records," "public disclosures," "public officials financial disclosure."

To learn of the details of a state's public records law, one can Google the state name along with the keyword, "public records law." It is possible that a given state will have no requirement for public officials to file financial disclosures. It is also possible that some states only have available the results of ethics investigations. For a clear answer on the issue, one might need to peruse a given state's public records law or contact the public records office with a request for the information of interest, or clarification of that state's public records law as such applies to the financial disclosures of public officials.

Whereas state laws vary on public officials' financial disclosures, with many states not requiring such filings, numerous states offer some ready access for the public to view campaign finance filings. Even though public servant financial disclosures are filed on behalf of individuals, these documents may disclose involvements in organizations other than the state agency with which the individual is employed by election, appointment, or some other hiring process. In contrast to the individual nature of public servant financial filings, campaign finance filings can be on behalf of individuals, including those running for office, those donating to campaigns of individuals, or those campaigning in support of a particular ballot referendum. The campaign finance filings can also be on behalf of organizations such as political action committees (PACs), labor unions, or corporations.

In order to find campaign finance reports, one could Google the state name along with the keyword, "campaign finance," "campaign reports," or "campaign reports search." For example, I just Googled, "Georgia campaign finance" and immediately found a link for the Georgia Government Transparency and Campaign Finance Commission's campaign reports search engine,[137] which I could use to search for campaign filings for either candidates or "non-candidate committees," including:

1. PACs,
2. Individual or corporate donors,
3. Ballot questions, or
4. Independent committees[138] that advertise in support of or against a candidate but do not directly donate to the candidate.

As is true of utilizing nonprofit tax forms to research individuals and organizations, researching campaign finance reports could fill a book by itself. Even though I cannot possibly exhaust the subject in this brief tutorial, I hope to offer readers useful, real-world examples of the utility of consulting campaign finance disclosures. Moreover, as I suggested for the section on nonprofit tax forms, readers may find it helpful to actually consult the campaign finance reports that I reference in end notes as they read about these examples in order to gain a better grasp of the associated campaign finance report examples discussed.

Perusal of campaign finance reports provides an opportunity for the public to become educated on the otherwise clandestine goings-on of corporate ed reformers in influencing politics to their liking, even in states in which they themselves do not reside. As an example, let us consider the November 2016 Massachusetts ballot initiative to raise the charter school cap, which was known as Question 2 (Q2).[139]

On the Massachusetts campaign finance search page, I can access a drop-down menu for "ballot question committee reports."[140] There I am able to select a year (2016) and scroll down to "Question 2: An Act to Allow Fair Access to Public Charter Schools." Note that the ballot initiative name does not indicate that this is about raising the charter school cap even though that is what a "yes" vote would mean. Several committees are listed—one list is for committees in support, and another for committees opposed. One such committee in support of Q2 is simply named, "Yes on 2," and it collected a total of $710,100.

When I click on "committee reports"[141] for "Yes on 2" and then click on the "data" tab at the top of the page, I discover that this committee has two donor entries—one dated 07/15/16 for an individual located in Massachusetts who donated $100 "to fund account," and another,

dated 07/25/16, from Arkansas billionaire, Alice
Walton, for $710,000.

By selecting the "expenditures" drop-down
menu at the top of the page, I can see that on
09/02/16, almost all of the money in the account,
$703K, was donated to another PAC support-
ing "yes" on Q2, the Campaign for Fair Access
to Quality Public Schools, which reported total
2016 donor receipts of $2.4M.[142] The balance of
the "Yes on 2" funds were used to pay consulting
and compliance fees.

If I return to the top of the page and click
"correspondence," I have access to the "Yes on 2"
documents titled, "statement of organization,"
(07/13/16), "filing notice" (08/19/16), and "closing letter" (10/14/16). These documents provide
evidence that "Yes on 2" was created for Alice
Walton to make a single $710,000 donation
in support of raising the charter school cap in
Massachusetts, the bulk of this money ($703K)
then being transferred to another PAC supporting
"yes" on Q2. This situation highlights the reality that PACs can donate to other PACs, thereby
creating funding layers that, either by nature or
more likely by design, conceal donors if those
people viewing campaign finance reports limit
their investigation to those PACs with the largest
donations and do not consider the possibility of
such funding layers.

Alice Walton's brother, Jim, also donated
$1,125,000 to the "Campaign for Fair Access to
Quality Public Schools." Unlike his sister, Jim

Walton made a direct donation. Thus, the two Waltons, both Arkansas residents, donated a combined $1,835,000 to increase charter schools in Massachusetts.

So, there we have Massachusetts campaign finance disclosure enabling the public to see that two Arkansas billionaires had donated the better part of two million dollars to raise the Massachusetts charter school cap, and allowing the public to know this prior to the November 2016 election. I was able to access all this information in September 2016, at which time I blogged about it.[143]

Of the out-of-state money coming into Massachusetts to try to raise the charter school cap in 2016 via Q2, perusal of Massachusetts' Q2 ballot question reports also shows that the New York based 501(c)(4) nonprofit, Families for Excellent Schools Advocacy (FESA)—a related organization to the 501(c)(3) nonprofit, Families for Excellent Schools (FES)—donated $15.3M to the ballot committee, Great Schools Massachusetts.

Following investigation of FESA donor records and subsequent FESA donations to Great Schools Massachusetts, the Massachusetts Office of Campaign and Political Finance (OCPF) fined FESA $426,500 for using its nonprofit status to conceal the identities of individual donors, thus violating Massachusetts' campaign finance disclosure laws. Moreover, in accordance with OCPF findings, FESA agreed to dissolve, and FES agreed to not operate in Massachusetts for four years.[144] In February 2018, FES chose to also disband[145] within a week of firing its CEO, Jeremiah Kittredge, over harassment allegations.[146]

Despite the out-of-state millions promoting "yes" on Q2, on November 08, 2016, Massachusetts voters soundly rejected expanding the charter school presence in their state, 62% to 38%.[147]

The out-of-state millionaire/billionaire ed reform presence is not limited to ballot initiatives. It is also present in elections. Let us consider the campaign finances associated with Louisiana's 2011 and 2015 Board of Elementary and Secondary Education (BESE) elections. By Googling "Louisiana campaign finance," I find a link to "view reports."[148] Once I click on "scanned reports," I can access a search engine for both filers and committees by using full or partial names.

Let us consider one BESE member who was elected in 2011 and re-elected in 2015, Teach for America executive director, Kira Orange-Jones.[149] A search for "kira orange" produces an active link for Orange-Jones.[150] By clicking on the link, I now have access to all of Orange-Jones' campaign filings from 2011 to 2019 (the time of this writing). If, for example, I click on the PDF report for 2011 "30 days before primary,"[151] I see that Orange-Jones reported $92K in contributions for 01/01/11 to 09/12/11. That's a lot of money for a BESE campaign.

However, what is not on this report are the names of the contributors. So, if I return to the "view reports" link,[152] I can choose the link, "campaign finance contributions"[153] and then search "kira orange jones." What I then see are a number of PDF files for documents listing Orange-Jones' donors. The page also defaults to listing the donors of the largest contributions across all of Orange-Jones' campaigns. For example, from this listing I can see at first glance that:

1. Santa Cruz, California, billionaire and Netflix CEO, Reed Hastings,
2. Los Angeles billionaire Eli Broad, and
3. Former New York mayor Michael Bloomberg.

Each donated at least $5,000 to Orange-Jones' 2011 campaign. Now I could peruse the entire list for multiple entries by each of these individuals, or I could conduct an advanced search of say, Michael Bloomberg's contributions to Orange-Jones' campaigns. By conducting the advanced search[154] of Bloomberg money to Orange-Jones— with "filer name" as "Orange-Jones, Kira" and "contributor's name" as "Michael Bloomberg"—I discover that Bloomberg actually made two separate contributions of $5K each (totaling $10K) to Orange-Jones' 2011 campaign and one $5K contribution to her 2015 campaign.

The tricky part in discovering the influence of out-of-state money on an election is in locating the PACs serving as "independent committees." These PACs can either promote or oppose a candidate or ballot measure while not directly contributing to any campaign. In the case of the 2015 BESE election, one such PAC was Empower

Louisiana, Inc., operated by Louisiana business-man, Lane Grigsby.[155]

One means of discovery is to conduct a search for all recipients of known out-of-state contributors. For example, since I learned that Michael Bloomberg had donated to Orange-Jones' campaign, I could conduct a search for all Louisiana campaign contributions made by Bloomberg. Such a search reveals Bloomberg's direct contributions to other BESE members' campaigns as well as to a number of Louisiana PACs, including Empower Louisiana. A similar search of Eli Broad also yields Empower Louisiana as one of the results. Thus, it seems logical to investigate Empower Louisiana's filings to see who or what the PAC supports or opposes and who else contributes to it.

As it so happens, Empower Louisiana supported 2015 BESE candidates who were more likely to promote market-based ed reform and opposed candidates less likely to do so. One example of how this independent expenditure process works is illustrated by Empower Louisiana's October 14, 2015, filing. Bloomberg donated $800,000 to the PAC, which was used to purchase television and radio ads on behalf of four BESE candidates.[156]

Another more remarkable example is Empower Louisiana's post-election filing, dated February 16, 2016.[157] Four BESE candidates are listed, and Empower Louisiana stood in favor of two and in opposition of the other two. Bloomberg donated another $650,000, bringing his total 2015 Empower Louisiana contributions to $1.45M. Broad donated $250K, Alice Walton donated $200K, and Jim Walton donated $450K. A total of $2.35M was donated to the Louisiana PAC by the four of them, which was used to purchase television, radio, and direct-mail ads and "media placement" such as billboards.

The goal of these out-of-state contributors to Empower Louisiana was to produce a Louisiana education board majority sympathetic to corporate-styled education reforms, including charter schools, and to keep ed reform-sympathetic state superintendent John White in office. For the most part, the out-of-state, billionaire money pump worked. In November 2015, 7 out of 11 BESE seats were won by ed reform-friendly candidates,[158] which allowed White to remain state superintendent, though without a renewed contract. For that, he needed a BESE supermajority, 8 out of 11 BESE votes.[159]

LITIGATION

A number of my inquiries into education issues have involved consulting court filings, including lawsuits and judicial decisions. Even though plaintiffs and defendants can certainly be individuals, I have included discussion of court filings in this section on organizations because a person suing an individual is often also suing the organization to which the individual belongs and for which the individual was a representative in the circumstances related to the suit.

Sometimes, my attention is drawn to a particular case because the case is in the news and therefore already has reporting being done about it. In such situations, in my efforts to view the actual court filings, I first see if any news outlets have linked to the case itself. If so, then I have access to the case, which means I also know the exact names of the named plaintiff(s) and defendant(s)—usually the first name of each, separated by "versus"—as well as the specific court in which the case was filed and the judge(s) presiding. More importantly, if I want to seek further information about the case from viewing a firsthand court document, I also have the case number.

If I cannot locate the court filings via links in news articles about the case, I seek to learn the names of primary plaintiffs, defendants, presiding courts/judges, and I Google these in combination—for example, plaintiff's name with judge's name, plaintiff's name with defendant's name—adding the keyword, "pdf" to help rule out articles that simply discuss the case, and also to increase my chances of locating the actual court filing. Note that this Googling sometimes produces related court documents such as petitions to introduce or limit information. Those documents are useful because they also include the case number, thereby allowing me to Google the case number and see what hits it produces.

Another means of locating cases is the legal site, Justia, and its search engine for locating dockets and filings.[160] I have found Justia useful because its basic search can be done using a plaintiff or defendant name, whether that is an individual or organization, as well as a judge's name. One can then scroll through hits to locate a case of interest. For example, in October 2015, *The New York Times* reported that Candido Brown, the principal of Success Academy of Fort Greene (New York), had created a "got to go list" of students he had seemingly targeted for removal from his school.[161]

Brown's decision resulted in litigation against him as well as organizations that he represented, including Success Academy of Fort Greene, Success Academy Charter Schools, Inc., and the New York State Education Department. If I Google "candido brown pdf," the first result (as of this writing) is an August 8, 2018, filing of the lawsuit.[162] Moreover, if I conduct a search of "candido brown" using Justia's search engine,[163] I find hits for two lawsuits. *Lawton et al. vs. Success Academy Charter Schools, Inc., et al.* (February 6, 2016) and *Ogundiran et al. vs. Success Academy Fort Greene et al.* (December 10, 2015).

By clicking on these lawsuits, I am able to immediately access some documents related to their history, including the August 8, 2018, filing I discovered in my initial, "candido brown pdf" Google search, which is related to the 2015,

Ogundiran suit. However, in order to access all of the documents of interest, I use an invaluable US government website, "Public Access to Court Electronic Records" (PACER).[164] This electronic public access service provided by the Federal Judiciary allows users to obtain case and docket information online from all federal appellate, district, and bankruptcy courts nationwide, including the Supreme Court of the United States (SCOTUS).[165]

The Justia site also provides a link for accessing PACER. Although one must sign up for the PACER service, it is so inexpensive that I have yet to exceed the $15-worth of free usage per quarter so as to incur a quarterly bill. In addition, via PACER, I am able to view an up-to-date history of all filings related to the case, which enables me to know that my information is complete.

Justia also offers easily accessible links to federal and state laws[166] as well as cases heard by the SCOTUS.[167] In order to seek original documents related to a SCOTUS decision, one can easily use the search feature on the Justia home page. For example, a search of the keyword "plessy" produced links to both *Plessy vs. Ferguson* (1896) and *Brown vs. Board* (1954). Note that this search is so general as to include a 2012 Arkansas case, *Plessy vs. State*, as well as other cases referencing the term, "plessy."[168]

Aside from using Justia, famous SCOTUS cases like *Plessy vs. Ferguson* can also be easily accessed by Googling "plessy vs. ferguson pdf." Finally, one can also access the official SCOTUS website and peruse the "opinions of the court."[169] Consider, however, that this "opinions" page has no search engine, so one must know the year a case was heard and decided by the SCOTUS. If one does not know specifics necessary to navigate the "opinions" page, one can use the SCOTUS "case citation finder"[170] to Google part of the case name, for example "board of education," to discover that there are actually five results, four of which relate to *Brown vs. Board of Education*, two in 1952 and two in 1954.

Thus, in the *Brown vs. Board* case, searching the SCOTUS "opinions of the court" would entail downloading archived files for 1952 and 1954 and digging in for a pre-internet-like, arguably tedious search of case documents. The advantage of such a search is that one can say one searched actual SCOTUS archives and that the search was comprehensive. Nevertheless, to conserve both time and effort, one may first access the SCOTUS case finder and then use the information gleaned to conduct a subsequent search of actual case files using Justia or PACER.

GLASSDOOR

When I am seeking insider information about an ed reform organization, one resource that I sometimes use is the online employment site, Glassdoor.[171] The site offers many services related to employment, including posting employee reviews for numerous organizations. One is able to read many of the reviews without joining the site. However, to extensively view the job reviews, one must join Glassdoor. A person may do so for no charge, but Glassdoor prompts those signing up to complete a profile. I have found that I can do so by offering as much or as little information as I choose, similar to the process I described in the section on the online resume site, LinkedIn.

What I appreciate about reading the employment reviews on Glassdoor is that the comments provide insights into education reform organizations and sometimes offer ideas for areas of further research that I might conduct on an organization and/or its leaders. One caution I offer is that since anyone can submit a review, it is possible for an organization to manipulate the reviews by asking select individuals to submit favorable reviews.

If an organization has a schism in its reviews whereby a number of reviews include similar negative sentiments, such as "no work-life balance" or "management does not hear us," and then in a short space of time, there are numerous positive reviews that read like promotional ads, one might conclude that those stellar reviews are probably not authentic. Nevertheless, even such "review padding" tells a story and teaches a lesson about the company—the organization is likely aware of negative reviews, apparently knows people read them, and is seemingly concerned about selling an image.

In signing on for a Glassdoor account, an individual agrees not to reproduce the reviews elsewhere. Thus, a downside of using Glassdoor is that as a researcher and writer about ed reform, I am unfortunately unable to copy and paste reviews so that my readers can see them for themselves. That noted, what I can do is provide the identifier for a given review and paraphrase the content. This way, my readers can go to the Glassdoor site and locate the actual review for themselves if they so choose. For example, I found a review for Success Academy Charter Schools (SA)[172] dated June 25, 2019 entitled, "Too Many Non Art Tasks," in which the reviewer notes that while SA budgets well for art supplies and even holds major art shows at schools twice per year, a substantial part of the art teacher's job is after-hours completion of math and English test preparation (including on weekends) and monthly test proctoring, making for 55- to 70-hour work weeks.

On Glassdoor, the organization also has the opportunity to respond to the reviews. Another SA review, dated June 17, 2019, and entitled, "Seriously Consider Before Working Here," focuses on teacher burnout and adds that the expected teacher stay at SA is 18 months. The SA response reads like an advertisement, painting SA as a place for enthusiastic go-getters, stating that the SA classroom career is not for everybody, and acknowledging that SA knows employee turnover is a problem that they are addressing. What

I noted from this response is that SA did not deny the reviewer's statement about the average SA teacher stay being 18 months, which lends credibility to the reviewer's information on just how quickly average SA teachers exit the SA classroom.

RECORDS REQUESTS FOR CONTRACTS

Previously in this book, I noted the usefulness of Freedom of Information Act (FOIA) or "public records" request for obtaining emails of public officials. I would like to extend my discussion of the utility of records requests to obtaining copies of contracts for the business relationships entered into by public agencies, including local school boards.

An example of my placing a public request with a public entity was my July 2017 request submitted to the Chicago Public Schools (CPS) FOIA Center[173] for "All contracts between Chicago Public Schools and Teach for America (TFA) for the years 2002–2007." It is worth noting that even though I reside in another state, I was still able to place this CPS FOIA request.

Once I filed my request, CPS sent an acknowledgement email stating that it had received my request and would respond within five days. However, the request took nine days. It seems that one contract for 2003 "could not be located with a reasonable search within the legal department."

If I had really needed that particular contract, I could have submitted another request explaining its importance and asking for any related documents, including email communications between CPS and TFA. As it stands, the remaining contracts provided a sufficient sense of the TFA presence in CPS for the number of years that Louisiana state education superintendent, John White, had served as Chicago's TFA executive director, which was the point of my research.

The federal government also has its own site, FOIA.gov, which is the Office of Information Policy at the US Department of Justice.[174] It is important to know which public agency holds the information of interest, and in some cases, multiple public agencies might have the information.

For example, Louisiana's Every Student Succeeds Act (ESSA) application is submitted to the US Department of Education (USDOE) and should be available to the public from both the USDOE and the Louisiana Department of Education, which raises another timesaving issue. Prior to submitting a public records request, check federal, state, and (when applicable) local agency websites, to see if any information of interest is already posted for public viewing. If there is any doubt, one could submit a FOIA request, and if the information is already available, the FOIA response officer would likely identify in the FOIA response exactly where one might find the document of interest.

FEDERAL AND STATE-LEVEL DATA

There are situations in which researchers may desire access to both federal and state level data. If one's research touches on education, a good starting point for federal level data on public and private schools, school districts, and international assessments, is the National Center for Education Statistics (NCES).[175] The NCES site includes a search feature. So, for example, when I entered, "cohort graduation rate," the search yielded a number of results,[176] including a report entitled, "Trends in High School Dropout and Completion Rates in the United States,"[177] which offers state-level information about the four-year graduation rates for 2015-16—in other words, the four-year graduation rate of high school students who were first-time freshmen in 2012-13.

For education data collected at the state level, one need only Google the name of the specific state along with the keyword, "school data," to view hits for accessing the state's school and district data sites. One example of how I used state level school data involved my February 2019 examination of the economic and ethnic demographics of Lycée Français de la Nouvelle-Orléans (Lycée Français), a French immersion charter school located in New Orleans.[178] The school was criticized in 2012 for having a notably wealthier, whiter student body than is representative of New Orleans students in general. I wanted to see if the situation remained the same six years later using

2018 data, the most recently available data at the time. In researching for my post, I accessed the October 2018 student demographic data from the Louisiana Department of Education (LDOE) "data center" website,[179] in order to compare the school's economic and ethnic demographics with that of the school district.

The following is a summary of my findings:

Lycée Français has been criticized in [2012] for both its predominately white student body and higher socioeconomic draw. …

Six years later (October 2018), of the 824 students enrolled at Lycée Français, 477 (58%) were white; 135 (16%) were black, and 130 (16%) were Hispanic.

According to October 2018 enrollment data, New Orleans schools in general served a student body that was 7% white (3,316 / 46,178) 82% black (37,977 / 46,178), 7% Hispanic (3,338 / 46,178).

As of October 2018, only 42% of Lycée Français's student body is economically disadvantaged, as compared with 83% of New Orleans students in general.

Thus, it is easy to see that the student body of New Orleans-based Lycée Français is not close to representing the general demographic of New Orleans students.[180]

My goal in examining demographic data for Lycée Français was to present to the public a concise analysis so that the public might know whether after several years, the Lycée Français' student body better resembled the city in which it operated. Based upon the LDOE economic and ethnic data, it did not.

Even though the LDOE demographic data comes in the form of extensive Excel spread sheets, in my post I chose to link directly to those spread sheets so that anyone who wished to do so could not only check the veracity of my conclusions, but also realize that as members of the public, they too have direct and ready access to such information about their schools—an empowering thought!

EARNINGS CALLS

A final source of organization-level information that I will highlight is the corporate earnings call. Earnings calls are periodic meetings that publicly traded companies hold with market analysts, investors, and interested members of the public for the purpose of discussing the company's financial position and performance.[181] To find out if a company is publicly traded, one could Google the name of the company with the term, "stock." If the query produces information on the trading price, the value of the company's stock, or the stock symbol used to represent the company in the stock market, then the company is publicly traded. Where there is a publicly-traded company there are earnings calls, and more importantly, earnings calls transcripts.

My principal use of earnings call transcripts has been in my research related to the United Kingdom (UK) based education publishing and testing giant, Pearson (stock market abbreviation PLC), which also operates around the world, including in the United States. Pearson has quarterly earnings calls, and the first Pearson earnings call transcript that I accessed was from February 28, 2014.[182] My interest at the time was in Pearson's plans to abundantly profit from the Common Core State Standards (CCSS) in the United States. By that time, Pearson had been chosen to deliver a major CCSS-related testing component, the Partnership for Assessment of Readiness for College and Career (PARCC) assessments. Thus, I was seeking to know what exactly Pearson executives had said to investors regarding the money-making promise of CCSS in the USA.

The earnings call transcript that I located was produced by a company called Seeking Alpha.[183] To locate such transcripts, one can Google the company name with the keywords, "earnings calls transcript" or "earnings calls seeking alpha." The result might be a listing by date, most recent first, of a number of earnings call transcripts for the publicly-traded company of interest. While I could have transcribed the entire earnings call myself, I chose not to do so because I had no particular interest in capturing speaker tone or voice inflection. Seeking Alpha allows users to directly quote up to 400 words from its earnings calls transcriptions so long as one includes a reference to Seeking Alpha in posting, and in this instance such conditions were worth the time I saved in not transcribing the meeting myself. The Seeking Alpha site does require one to sign up by creating a username and password. This is the course I chose—signing up, quoting 400 words max, and citing Seeking Alpha—when I published my May 20, 2014, post about Pearson's February 28, 2014, earnings call.[184]

What struck me most about this earnings call was this—when pressed by an analyst about Pearson's plans if CCSS did not produce the profits the company was counting on, Pearson CEO John Fallon offered no alternative course of action. In answering questions posed by a second analyst, Fallon dismissed the idea of educators accessing open platforms. He just knew CCSS would be profitable because Pearson planned to embed its CCSS products into American education. By the time I had reached this point in my post, I had used up my 400 words. As much as I would like to directly quote from the transcript in this book, I cannot do so because I have already reached my word limit for this particular earnings call in my other writings. (For more on Pearson's history and CCSS hopes, see chapter 11 of my book, *Common Core Dilemma*.[185])

Reading Pearson's earnings call transcript allowed me to gain some insight into CEO Fallon's

CCSS profit certainty, a certainty that he was willing to underscore in discussing Pearson's financial position and projections. However, Fallon had too much faith in CCSS profits bolstering Pearson. PARCC as a dominant CCSS assessment literally fell apart. States dropped out to such a degree that within five years of that 2014 earnings call, by 2019, PARCC was allowing states to choose their own testing vendors while still using PARCC items.[186] Even prior to that, by 2017, PARCC itself was offering an annual PARCC test managed and developed by another vendor, New Meridian Corporation. As of this writing, on the PARCC "about" page, Pearson is not even mentioned as part of the PARCC history.[187]

With the satisfying image of testing giant Pearson being dealt a blow by the very market that education reform is pushing onto traditional public education, I will conclude what I hope has been a fruitful and informative journey into how I conduct my research.

CONCLUDING THIS PEDAGOGIC JOURNEY

This book began with my thinking about what I would include in a book to equip parents and other community members with some tools to investigate the activities and spending of individuals and groups associated with ed reform. At the 2018 Network for Public Education (NPE) conference in Indianapolis,[188] my colleagues Andrea Gabor, Darcie Cimarusti, and I made a presentation on tracking the funding related to the promotion of market-based education reform titled, "Where Did All This Money Come From??: Locating and Following the Dark Money Trail."[189] In preparing for our presentation, Darcie asked me to send her the information I wished to include on my presentation slides.

In that moment, I thought, "To do this justice, my slides would need to be the length of a book. And there's no time for me to write a book before we present."

So, the book was on my mind, particularly on one Saturday after the 2018 NPE. At future conferences in which I might speak about how I conduct my research, I wanted to be able to offer participants my thoughts in book form.

I am pleased to note this is that book—the book in which I canvassed my own research writings and questioned myself about how I accomplish my research. I also quizzed myself about how to effectively communicate my research knowledge and experience to readers who may have little to no research experience, with the goal of empowering them. Moreover, after writing this book and considering the many lessons I have included in it, I knew that the referenced skills, strategies, and advice could provide valuable guidance for researchers in numerous settings and addressing a variety of research questions.

Empowering researchers to confront market-based education reform tactics and wiles, and beyond.

I'm happy to do both.

REFERENCES

1   Public Law 107-110. (2002, January 8). [Legislation].
    Retrieved from https://www2.ed.gov/policy/elsec/leg/
    esea02/107-110.pdf

2   Schneider, Mercedes K. (2018, November 20).
    Louisiana teacher arrested at January 2018 meeting
    vindicated by judge's ruling [Web blog post].
    Retrieved from https://deutsch29.wordpress.
    com/2018/11/20/louisiana-teacher-arrested-at-
    january-2018-board-meeting-vindicated-by-judges-
    ruling/

3   Layton, Lyndsey. (2014, June 10). California court
    rules teacher tenure creates impermissible, unequal
    conditions. *The Washington Post.* Retrieved from
    https://www.washingtonpost.com/local/education/
    calif-court-rules-teacher-tenure-creates-unequal-
    conditions/2014/06/10/8be4f64a-f0be-11e3-914c-
    1fbd0614e2d4_story.html?utm_term=.c703045b78ed

4   Layton, Lyndsey. (2014, June 7). How Bill Gates
    pulled off the swift Common Core revolution. *The
    Washington Post.* Retrieved from https://www.
    washingtonpost.com/politics/how-bill-gates-pulled-
    off-the-swift-common-core-revolution/2014/06/07/
    a830e32e-ec34-11e3-9f5c-9075d5508f0a_story.
    html?utm_term=.a0757057579a

5   Schneider, Mercedes K. (2015). *Common Core
    Dilemma: Who Owns Our Schools?* New York:
    Teachers College Press.

6   Alemany, Jacqueline. (2018, June 13). Sarah Sanders,
    Raj Shah planning to depart the White House. *CBS*

News. Retrieved from https://www.cbsnews.com/
news/sarah-sanders-raj-shah-planning-to-depart-the-
white-house/

7   Fenwick, Cody. (2018, December 30). Sarah Sanders
has "struggled' to find new job as the White House
press office becomes "night of the living dead":
report. *AlterNet.* Retrieved from https://www.
rawstory.com/2018/12/sarah-sanders-struggled-find-
new-job-white-house-press-office-becomes-night-
living-dead-report/

8   @realDonaldTrump. (2019, June 13). "After 3 1/2
years, our wonderful Sarah Huckabee Sanders will
be leaving the White House at the end of the month
and going home to the Great State of Arkansas...."
[Twitter posting]. Retrieved from https://twitter.com/
realDonaldTrump/status/1139263781144596486

9   Green, Elizabeth. (2010, March 1). We read the
Moskowitz/Klein e-mails so that you don't have to.
Chalkbeat. Retrieved from https://www.chalkbeat.org/
posts/ny/2010/03/01/we-read-the-moskowitzklein-e-
mails-so-that-you-dont-have-to/

10   Schneider, Mercedes K. (2014). Eva Moskowitz:
Stage Mother of Charter School Success [Book
chapter]. In *A Chronicle of Echoes: Who's Who in the
Implosion of American Public Education.* Charlotte,
NC: Information Age Press.

11   FOIA Advocates. (2019). Frequently asked questions.
Retrieved from http://www.foiadvocates.com/faq.html

12   Louisiana Department of Education. (n.d.).
Resources: contact us. Retrieved January 01, 2019,
from https://www.louisianabelieves.com/resources/
contact-us

13   Schneider, Mercedes K. (2018, April 16). For-
profit SPEDx's end-game: Cut services for a lower
bottom line [Web blog post]. Retrieved from https://
deutsch29.wordpress.com/2018/04/16/for-profit-
spedxs-end-game-cut-sped-services-for-a-lower-
bottom-line/

14   Schneider, Mercedes K. (2015). *Common Core
Dilemma: Who Owns Our Schools?* New York:

Teachers College Press.

15   Schneider, Mercedes K. (2015). The "State-Led" Lock-In [Book chapter]. In *Common Core Dilemma: Who Owns Our Schools?* New York: Teachers College Press.

16   Schneider, Mercedes K. (2015). *Common Core Dilemma: Who Owns Our Schools?* New York: Teachers College Press.

17   Education Trust. (2019). Kati Haycock [biographical sketch]. Retrieved from https://edtrust.org/team/kati-haycock/

18   Education Trust. (2014, July 03). About: senior leadership: Kati Haycock [Archived biographical sketch]. Retrieved from https://web.archive.org/web/20140703233030/http://www.edtrust.org/dc/about/senior-leadership

19   Schneider, Mercedes K. (2015). Playing in the Achieve sandbox: Education Trust and Fordham Institute [Book chapter]. In *Common Core Dilemma: Who Owns Our Schools?* New York: Teachers College Press.

20   Bill and Melinda Gates Foundation. (2012, June). American Federation of Teachers Education Foundation [grants search engine result]. Retrieved from https://www.gatesfoundation.org/How-We-Work/Quick-Links/Grants-Database/Grants/2012/06/OPP1060566

21   Weingarten, Randi. (2010, November). Foreword. In Harris, Douglas N. (2011). *Value-Added Measures in Education: What Every Educator Needs to Know.* Cambridge, MA: Harvard University Press. Retrieved from https://www.amazon.com/Value-Added-Measures-Education-Every-Educator/dp/1612500005

22   Burris, Carol. (2015, January 9). If you can't trust your union… [Article on the website of the Port Jefferson Station Teachers Association]. Retrieved from https://thepjsta.org/2015/01/09/if-you-cant-trust-your-union/

23   Schneider, Mercedes K. (2014, November 14).

Weingarten hearts Cuomo by proxy to undercut Teachout via last-minute robocall [Web blog post]. Retrieved from https://deutsch29.wordpress.com/2014/09/14/weingarten-hearts-cuomo-by-proxy-willing-to-undercut-teachout-via-last-minute-robocall/

24 Schneider, Mercedes K. (2014). *A Chronicle of Echoes: Who's Who in the Implosion of American Public Education.* Charlotte, NC: Information Age Press.

25 Barrett, Wayne. (2003, May 13). Weingarten's war. *Village Voice.* Retrieved from https://www.villagevoice.com/2003/05/13/weingartens-war/

26 Schneider, Mercedes K. (2014). The Aspen and Pahara Institutes: Advancing privatization in fine style [Book chapter]. In *A Chronicle of Echoes: Who's Who in the Implosion of American Public Education.* Charlotte, NC: Information Age Press.

27 New York State Education Department. (n.d.). Teacher certification lookup [Search engine]. Retrieved from http://eservices.nysed.gov/teach/certhelp/CpPersonSearchExternal.jsp

28 Gleason, Beth. (2011, November). Update on value-added/Act 54 information [Louisiana Department of Education presentation.] Retrieved from https://www.louisianabelieves.com/docs/default-source/links-for-newsletters/lft-presentation-nov-20111.pdf

29 National Comprehensive Center for Teacher Quality. (2012, September). Conference presenter biographies. Retrieved from https://gtlcenter.org/sites/default/files/docs/TQ_Conf_Bios.pdf

30 Louisiana Department of Education. (n.d.). Compass. Retrieved May 2019 from http://www.louisianabelieves.com/academics/compass

31 Louisiana Department of Education. (n.d.). Verify certificate or teaching authorization [Search engine]. Retrieved from https://www.teachlouisiana.net/teachers.aspx?PageID=416

32 Schneider, Mercedes K. (2013, March 27). Former TFAers-Gone-LDOE-Leaders: Incompetence at a

Premium [Web blog post]. Retrieved from https:// deutsch29.wordpress.com/2013/03/27/former-tfaers-gone-ldoe-leaders-incompetence-at-a-premium/

33   Sentell, Will. (2012, September 29). Evaluator defends not renewing own teacher certificate. Baton Rouge *Advocate*. Retrieved from https://web.archive. org/web/20121119123850/https://www.theadvocate. com/home/4004848-125/evaluator-defends-not-renewing-own/

34   Schneider, Mercedes K. (2015, September 18). A Molly Horstman update [Web blog post]. Retrieved from https://deutsch29.wordpress.com/2015/09/18/a-molly-horstman-update/

35   Schneider, Mercedes K. (2014, November 24). Who is New York-Regents-Charter-Approved Ted J. Morris, Jr.? [Web blog post]. Retrieved from https:// deutsch29.wordpress.com/2014/11/24/who-is-new-york-regents-charter-approved-ted-j-morris-jr/

36   Schneider, Mercedes K. (2017, July 9). John White forgot something on several years of ethics disclosures: His wife [web blog post]. Retrieved from https://deutsch29.wordpress.com/2017/07/09/john-white-forgot-something-on-several-years-of-ethics-disclosures-his-wife/

37   Schneider, Mercedes K. (2017, July 12). John White and Katherine Westerhold [Web blog post]. Retrieved from https://deutsch29.wordpress.com/2017/07/12/ john-white-and-katherine-westerhold/

38   Schneider, Mercedes K. (2017, December 19). La. Supt. John White seeks ethics advice on business connections to wife, Katherine Westerhold [Web blog post]. Retrieved from https://deutsch29.wordpress. com/2017/12/19/la-supt-john-white-seeks-ethics-advice-on-business-connections-to-wife-katherine-westerhold/

39   Schneider, Mercedes K. (2013, March 27). Former TFAers-Gone-LDOE-Leaders: Incompetence at a Premium [Web blog post]. Retrieved from https:// deutsch29.wordpress.com/2013/03/27/former-tfaers-gone-ldoe-leaders-incompetence-at-a-premium/

40   Schneider, Mercedes K. (2018, June 24). TFAer Rebecca Kockler leaves Louisiana to work her wonders in Los Angeles [Web blog post]. Retrieved from https://deutsch29.wordpress.com/2018/06/24/tfaer-rebecca-kockler-leaves-louisiana-to-work-her-wonders-in-los-angeles/

41   Schneider, Mercedes K. (2015). *Common Core Dilemma: Who Owns Our Schools?* New York: Teachers College Press.

42   Illinois State Board of Education. (2007, November 14-15). Board meeting minutes. Retrieved from https://web.archive.org/web/20111121053740/http://www.isbe.net/board/meetings/2007/nov07/2007-11.pdf

43   Louisiana Department of Education. (2016). U.S. Department of Education application for grants under the FY2016 TIF Competition 84.374A: Office of Innovation and Improvement OII): Teacher incentive fund. Retrieved from https://www2.ed.gov/programs/teacherincentive/fy16/lousianadoe.pdf

44   Barkan, Joanne. (2017, Spring). The miseducation of Betsy DeVos. *Dissent Magazine.* Retrieved from https://www.dissentmagazine.org/article/miseducation-betsy-devos-public-schools

45   U.S. Department of Education. (2019, June 27). Betsy DeVos, secretary of education-- biography. Retrieved from https://www2.ed.gov/news/staff/bios/devos.html

46   Schneider, Mercedes K. (2017, March 31). Betsy DeVos' mother's brief stint as a public school teacher: Some details [Web blog post]. Retrieved from https://deutsch29.wordpress.com/2017/03/31/betsy-devos-mothers-brief-stint-as-a-public-school-teacher-some-details/

47   Schneider, Mercedes K. (2014). *A Chronicle of Echoes: Who's Who in the Implosion of American Public Education.* Charlotte, NC: Information Age Press.

48   New York State United Teachers. (n.d.). Shanker library. Retrieved June 2019 from https://www.nysut.org/resources/special-resources-sites/social-justice/

shanker-library

49   U.S. Department of Education. (2016, January 27).
      Speech archive for Arne Duncan and John King.
      Retrieved from https://www.ed.gov/news/speech-
      archive?page=2

50   Internet Archive. (n.d.). Wayback machine [Internet
      archive search engine]. Retrieved from https://
      archive.org/web/

51   Google. (2019). View web pages cached in Google
      search results. Retrieved from https://support.google.
      com/websearch/answer/1687222?hl=en

52   Schneider, Mercedes K. (2019, May 19). Jeanne Allen
      and her Center for Education Reform [Web blog
      post]. Retrieved from https://deutsch29.wordpress.
      com/2019/05/19/jeanne-allen-and-her-center-for-
      education-reform-cer/

53   Quora. (2017, October 9). What is a web crawler and
      how does it work [Discussion board]. Retrieved from
      https://www.quora.com/What-is-a-web-crawler-and-
      how-does-it-work

54   Walker, Dave. (2013, February 6). OWN's
      Blackboard Wars" aims its cameras at John
      McDonogh High School. *The Times-Picayune.*
      Retrieved from https://www.nola.com/entertainment_
      life/movies_tv/article_37f461e5-5059-59df-87d9-
      a6cb1eea2339.html

55   Dreilinger, Danielle. (214, January 17). John
      McDonogh High School, "Blackboard Wars" focus,
      will close in June. *The Times-Picayune.* Retrieved
      from https://www.nola.com/news/education/
      article_1ddccce2-8480-52a8-bc6d-c3b43bf2c210.
      html

56   Vanacore, Andrew. (2011, April 9). John White wins
      approval to lead Recovery School District in New
      Orleans. *The Times-Picayune.* Retrieved from https://
      www.nola.com/news/education/article_9a4b3191-
      da92-5fd1-85b9-b8c7554551da.html

57   Hess, Rick. (2012, February 6). Straight up
      conversation: New Louisiana schools chief John

White. *Education Week.* Retrieved from http://blogs.
edweek.org/edweek/rick_hess_straight_up/2012/02/
straight_up_conversation_new_louisiana_schools_
chief_john_white.html

58   Hasselle, Della. (2018, September 2). Old John
       McDonogh High School building gets transformation
       as Bricolage moves in. *The New Orleans Advocate.*
       Retrieved from https://www.theadvocate.com/new_
       orleans/news/education/article_26aeb5ee-ad67-11e8-
       a561-1710ee244067.html

59   Schneider, Mercedes K. (2016). *School Choice:
       The End of Public Education?* New York: Teachers
       College Press.

60   Doherty, Brian. (1995, June). Best of both worlds: An
       interview with Milton Friedman. *Reason.* Retrieved
       from https://reason.com/1995/06/01/best-of-both-
       worlds/

61   Schneider, Mercedes K. (2016). Milton Friedman
       and his unrealistic school choice [Book chapter].
       In *School Choice: The End of American Public
       Education?* Charlotte, NC: Information Age Press.

62   Schneider, Mercedes K. (2015, October 31). Alabama
       teacher of the year abruptly resigns [Web blog
       post]. Retrieved from https://deutsch29.wordpress.
       com/2015/10/31/2014-15-alabama-teacher-of-the-
       year-abruptly-resigns/

63   Schneider, Mercedes K. (2016, January 14). Alabama
       teacher of the year, Ann Marie Corgill: Reflecting and
       dreaming [Web blog post]. Retrieved from https://
       deutsch29.wordpress.com/2016/01/14/alabama-
       teacher-of-the-year-ann-marie-corgill-reflecting-and-
       dreaming/

64   Schneider, Mercedes K. (2016, January 26). Ashana
       Bigard: An insider's view of post-Katrina New
       Orleans public education [Web blog post]. Retrieved
       from https://deutsch29.wordpress.com/2016/01/26/
       ashana-bigard-an-insiders-view-of-post-katrina-new-
       orleans-public-education/

65   BackpackFullofCash.com. (2019). About the film.
       Retrieved from https://www.backpackfullofcash.

com/#about-the-film

66   Shanahan, Mark. (2017, October 5). School-
     choice advocate says Damon-narrated film is
     backpack full of hypocrisy." *The Boston Globe.*
     Retrieved from https://www.bostonglobe.
     com/lifestyle/names/2017/10/05/matt-damon-
     public-school-documentary-called-hypocritical/
     TMTaFkw3cEBnatMHeF1FvN/story.html#comments

67   Schneider, Mercedes K. (2017, October 8). Jeanne
     Allen's beef with *Backpack Full of Cash* [Web blog
     post]. Retrieved from https://deutsch29.wordpress.
     com/2017/10/08/jeanne-allens-beef-with-backpack-
     full-of-cash/

68   Allen, Jeanne. (2017, October 10). *Backpack Full of
     Cash* is a false narrative funded by teachers' unions,
     created to bolster failing schools. *LinkedIn.* Retrieved
     from https://www.LinkedIn.com/pulse/backpack-full-
     cash-false-narrative-funded-teachers-unions-allen

69   U.S. Department of Education. (2016, January 27).
     Speech archive for Arne Duncan and John King.
     Retrieved from https://www.ed.gov/news/speech-
     archive?page=2 ; U.S. Department of Education
     (2017–2019). Speeches of Betsy DeVos. Retrieved
     from https://www.ed.gov/news/speeches

70   Bill and Melinda Gates Foundation. (n.d.). Press
     room: Speeches [Search engine]. Retrieved from
     https://www.gatesfoundation.org/Media-Center/
     Speeches

71   Schneider, Mercedes K. (2016, September 10).
     Arkansas residents Jim and Alice Walton pony up
     $1,835,000 to raise charter cap in Massachusetts
     [Web blog post]. Retrieved from https://deutsch29.
     wordpress.com/2016/09/10/arkansas-residents-jim-
     and-alice-walton-pony-up-1835000-to-raise-charter-
     cap-in-massachusetts/

72   Schneider, Mercedes K. (2014, May 13). College
     dropout Bill Gates—who spends millions on
     Harvard—gets honorary doctorate [Web blog
     post]. Retrieved from https://deutsch29.wordpress.
     com/2014/05/13/college-dropout-bill-gates-who-

spends-millions-on-harvard-gets-honorary-doctorate/

73   Lyndsey. (2014, June 7). How Bill Gates pulled off
      the swift Common Core revolution. *The Washington
      Post.* Retrieved from https://www.washingtonpost.
      com/politics/how-bill-gates-pulled-off-the-swift-
      common-core-revolution/2014/06/07/a830e32e-ec34-
      11e3-9f5c-9075d5508f0a_story.html?utm_term=.
      a0757057579a

74   Schneider, Mercedes K. (2013, August 27). A
      brief audit of Bill Gates' Common Core spending
      [Web blog post]. Retrieved from https://deutsch29.
      wordpress.com/2013/08/27/a-brief-audit-of-bill-gates-
      common-core-spending/

75   Schneider, Mercedes K. (2016, October 4). Gates
      Foundation money connects Common Core and ESSA
      [Web blog post]. Retrieved from https://deutsch29.
      wordpress.com/2016/10/04/gates-foundation-money-
      connects-common-core-and-essa/

76   Schneider, Mercedes K. (2014, May 13). College
      dropout Bill Gates—who spends millions on
      Harvard—gets honorary doctorate [Web blog
      post]. Retrieved from https://deutsch29.wordpress.
      com/2014/05/13/college-dropout-bill-gates-who-
      spends-millions-on-harvard-gets-honorary-doctorate/

77   Gates, Bill. (2009, July 21). National Conference of
      State Legislatures: Prepared remarks by Bill Gates,
      co-chair [speech]. Retrieved from https://www.
      gatesfoundation.org/media-center/speeches/2009/07/
      bill-gates-national-conference-of-state-legislatures-
      ncsl

78   Bill and Melinda Gates Foundation. (n.d.). National
      conference of state legislatures [Search engine
      result]. Retrieved June 2019 from https://www.
      gatesfoundation.org/How-We-Work/Quick-Links/
      Grants-Database#q/k=national%20conference%20
      of%20state%20legislatures

79   Layton, Lyndsey. (2014, June 7). How Bill Gates
      pulled off the swift Common Core revolution. *The
      Washington Post.* Retrieved from https://www.
      washingtonpost.com/politics/how-bill-gates-pulled-

off-the-swift-common-core-revolution/2014/06/07/
a830e32e-ec34-11e3-9f5c-9075d5508f0a_story.
html?utm_term=.a0757057579a

80 Gates, Bill. (2009, July 21). National Conference of
State Legislatures: Prepared remarks by Bill Gates,
co-chair [speech]. Retrieved from https://www.
gatesfoundation.org/media-center/speeches/2009/07/
bill-gates-national-conference-of-state-legislatures-
ncsl

81 Bill and Melinda Gates Foundation. (n.d.). Grants
database [Search engine]. Retrieved June 2019 from
https://www.gatesfoundation.org/How-We-Work/
Quick-Links/Grants-Database

82 Walton Family Foundation (n.d.) Grants database
[Search engine]. Retrieved June 2019 from https://
www.waltonfamilyfoundation.org/grants-database

83 American Federation for Children. (2016, November
30). Bill Oberndorf succeeds Betsy DeVos as
chairman of American Federation for Children
[Website post]. Retrieved from https://www.
federationforchildren.org/bill-oberndorf-succeeds-
betsy-devos-chairman-american-federation-children/

84 ProPublica. (n.d.) Nonprofit explorer: American
Federation for Children, Inc.: Form 990 for period
ending December 2004 [Search engine result].
Retrieved from https://projects.propublica.org/
nonprofits/display_990/330627955/2005_07_
EO%2F33-0627955_990O_200412

85 Walton Family Foundation (n.d.). Grants database:
American Federation for Children [Search engine
result]. Retrieved June 2019 from https://www.
waltonfamilyfoundation.org/grants-database?q=ameri
can+federation+for+children&s=1

86 Kagan, Julia. (2019, March 12). Employer
identification number (EIN). *Investopedia.* Retrieved
from https://www.investopedia.com/terms/e/
employer-identification-number.asp

87 Schneider, Mercedes K. (2015, October 29). The
Waltons set out to promote "choice ecosystems"
[Web blog post]. Retrieved from https://deutsch29.

wordpress.com/2015/10/29/2016-20-the-waltons-set-out-to-promote-choice-ecosystems/

88   Wilson, Michelle. (2015, October). Investing in Change: The Walton Family Foundation charts a new course [Report]. Retrieved from https://deutsch29.files.wordpress.com/2015/10/walton-2015-priorities.pdf

89   Schneider, Mercedes K. (2015, October 29). The Waltons set out to promote "choice ecosystems" [Web blog post]. Retrieved from https://deutsch29.wordpress.com/2015/10/29/2016-20-the-waltons-set-out-to-promote-choice-ecosystems/

90   Walton Family Foundation. (n.d.). About us: Newsroom. Retrieved June 2019 from https://www.waltonfamilyfoundation.org/about-us/newsroom

91   Walton Family Foundation. (n.d.). Our work: K-12 education. Retrieved June 2019 from https://www.waltonfamilyfoundation.org/our-work/k-12-education

92   Eli and Edythe Broad Foundation. (n.d.). Home page. Retrieved June 2019 from https://broadfoundation.org/

93   Max M. and Marjorie S. Fisher Foundation. (n.d.). Home page. Retrieved June 2019 from https://mmfisher.org/

94   Max M. and Marjorie S. Fisher Foundation. (n.d.). Grant partners. Retrieved June 2019 from https://mmfisher.org/grant-partners/

95   Internal Revenue Service. (n.d.). Public disclosure and availability of exempt organizations returns and applications: Public disclosure requirements in general. Retrieved July 4, 2019, from https://www.irs.gov/charities-non-profits/public-disclosure-and-availability-of-exempt-organizations-returns-and-applications-public-disclosure-requirements-in-general

96   Internal Revenue Service. (n.d.). Social welfare organizations. Retrieved July 4, 2019, from https://www.irs.gov/charities-non-profits/other-non-profits/social-welfare-organizations

97   Internal Revenue Service. (n.d.). EO operational requirements: Limitations on activities. Retrieved July 4, 2019, from https://www.irs.gov/charities-non-profits/eo-operational-requirements-limitations-on-activities

98   Internal Revenue Service. (n.d.). The restriction of political campaign intervention by section 501(c)(3) tax-exempt organizations. Retrieved July 4, 2019, from https://www.irs.gov/charities-non-profits/charitable-organizations/the-restriction-of-political-campaign-intervention-by-section-501c3-tax-exempt-organizations

99   Internal Revenue Service. (n.d.). Public disclosure and availability of exempt organizations returns and applications: Public disclosure overview. Retrieved July 4, 2019, from https://www.irs.gov/charities-non-profits/public-disclosure-and-availability-of-exempt-organization-returns-and-applications-public-disclosure-overview ; Internal Revenue Service. (2018). Schedule B (Form 990, 990-EZ, or 990-PF): Schedule of contributors. Retrieved July 4, 2019, from https://www.irs.gov/pub/irs-pdf/f990ezb.pdf

100 Internal Revenue Service. (n.d.). Tax exempt organization search [Search engine]. Retrieved July 4, 2019, from https://apps.irs.gov/app/eos/

101 Foundation Center. (2019). 990 finder [Search engine]. http://foundationcenter.org/find-funding/990-finder

102 ProPublica. (n.d.). Nonprofit explorer [Search engine]. Retrieved July 4, 2019, from https://projects.propublica.org/nonprofits/

103 Conservative Transparency. (2019). Basic search [Candidate, donor, and nonprofit search engine]. Retrieved from http://conservativetransparency.org/basic-search/

104 GuideStar. (2019). GuideStar products and services. Retrieved from https://learn.guidestar.org/products/

105 CitizenAudit. (2019). Home page. Retrieved from https://www.citizenaudit.org/

106 American Enterprise Institute for Public Policy
     Research. (2018). Form 990. Retrieved from
     https://projects.propublica.org/nonprofits/
     organizations/530218495/201823449349300307/
     IRS990

107 American Enterprise Institute for Public
     Policy Research. (2018). Form 990,
     Schedule J. Retrieved July 4, 2019, from
     https://projects.propublica.org/nonprofits/
     organizations/530218495/201823449349300307/
     IRS990ScheduleJ

108 American Enterprise Institute for Public Policy
     Research. (2017). Form 990. Retrieved from
     https://projects.propublica.org/nonprofits/
     organizations/530218495/201810169349300216/
     IRS990

109 American Enterprise Institute for Public
     Policy Research. (2018). Form 990,
     Schedule L. Retrieved July 4, 2019, from
     https://projects.propublica.org/nonprofits/
     organizations/530218495/201823449349300307/
     IRS990ScheduleL

110 American Enterprise Institute for Public
     Policy Research. (2018). Form 990,
     Schedule M. Retrieved July 4, 2019, from
     https://projects.propublica.org/nonprofits/
     organizations/530218495/201823449349300307/
     IRS990ScheduleM

111 American Enterprise Institute for Public Policy
     Research (2018). Form 990, Schedule R. Retrieved
     from https://projects.propublica.org/nonprofits/
     organizations/530218495/201823449349300307/
     IRS990ScheduleR

112 American Enterprise Institute for Public Policy
     Research. (2018). Form 990, Schedule O. Retrieved
     from https://projects.propublica.org/nonprofits/
     organizations/530218495/201823449349300307/
     IRS990ScheduleO

113 Education Trust. (2016). Form 990. Retrieved from
     http://990s.foundationcenter.org/990_pdf_arch

ive/521/521982223/521982223_201706_990.pdf

114   Data Quality Campaign. (2019). Who we are. Retrieved from https://dataqualitycampaign.org/who-we-are/

115   Success Academy Charter Schools, Inc. (2016). Form 990. Retrieved from https://projects.propublica.org/nonprofits/organizations/205298861/201731329349303718/IRS990

116   Success Foundation, Inc. (2016). Form 990. Retrieved from https://projects.propublica.org/nonprofits/organizations/461501902/201721329349303812/IRS990

117   Kolker, Robert. (2006, February 10). How is a hedge fund like a school? *New York Magazine.* Retrieved from http://nymag.com/news/businessfinance/15958/

118   LinkedIn. (n.d). Chuck Strauch [Resume]. Retrieved January 10, 2020, from https://www.linkedin.com/in/chuck-strauch-2510338

119   Schneider, Mercedes K. (2018, April 27). Hedge-fund backers pay Success Academy CEO Eva Moskowitz via special nonprofit [Web blog post]. Retrieved from https://deutsch29.wordpress.com/2018/04/27/hedge-fund-backers-pay-success-academy-ceo-eva-moskowitz-via-a-special-nonprofit/

120   Layton, Lyndsey. (2014, September 1). Education Post aims to take the sting out of national conversations about school reform. *The Washington Post.* Retrieved from https://www.washingtonpost.com/local/education/education-post-aims-to-take-the-sting-out-of-national-conversations-about-school-reform/2014/09/01/65f11832-2fb2-11e4-bb9b-997ae96fad33_story.html?utm_term=.da376c07e412

121   Schneider, Mercedes K. (2016, April 21). More about "Education Post, the Nonprofit"—including its anonymous donor [Web blog post]. Retrieved from https://deutsch29.wordpress.com/2016/04/21/more-about-education-post-the-nonprofit-including-its-anonymous-donor/

122   Education Post. (n.d.). About Education Post.
       Retrieved from https://educationpost.org/about/

123   Eli and Edythe Broad Foundation. (2014). Form 990-
       PF. Retrieved from https://deutsch29.files.wordpress.
       com/2016/04/95-4686318_990pf_201412.pdf

124   Emerson Collective. (2011, June 28). Articles of
       organization. State of California Secretary of State.
       Retrieved from https://businesssearch.sos.ca.gov/
       Document/RetrievePDF?Id=201118010057-13914122

125   Internal Revenue Service. (n.d.). Tax information for
       charities and other nonprofits. Retrieved July 4, 2019,
       from https://www.irs.gov/charities-non-profits

126   U.S. Small Business Administration. (n.d.). Register
       your business. Retrieved July , 2019, from https://
       www.sba.gov/business-guide/launch-your-business/
       register-your-business

127   Emerson Collective. (2019). Home page. Retrieved
       from https://www.emersoncollective.com/

128   Emerson Collective. (2019). Our mission. Retrieved
       from https://www.emersoncollective.com/about-us/

129   ProPublica. (n.d.). Full text search: Emerson
       Collective [Search engine result]. Retrieved June
       2019 from https://projects.propublica.org/nonprofits/
       full_text_search?utf8=%E2%9C%93&q=emerson+co
       llective

130   Bloomberg. (2018, August 15). Company
       overview of Emerson Collective LLC [Archived
       web page]. Retrieved from https://web.archive.
       org/web/20180815200611/https://www.
       bloomberg.com/research/stocks/private/snapshot.
       asp?privcapId=263956917

131   California Secretary of State. (2017). Business
       search [Search engine]. Retrieved from https://
       businesssearch.sos.ca.gov/

132   Ramsey County, Minnesota. (2013, May 21).
       Property tax bill for 1030 Como Avenue, Saint Paul,
       MN 55103-1021. Retrieved from https://beacon.
       schneidercorp.com/application.aspx?AppID=959&La
       yerID=18852&PageTypeID=4&PageID=8397&Q=17

6167618&KeyValue=262923220038

133   TenSquare. (2019). Our team. Retrieved from http://
      www.thetensquaregroup.com/about/our-team

134   DelawareInc.com. (2019). Seven major Delaware
      LLC advantages. Retrieved from https://www.
      delawareinc.com/llc/advantages-of-llc/

135   Manderscheid, Marc J. (2019, May 10). Submission
      by Twin Cities German Immersion School and
      Twin Cities German Immersion School Building
      Company opposing proposed Ordinance 19-1,
      designating the former St. Andrew Church
      building as a Saint Paul heritage preservation site
      [Letter to St. Paul, MN, city council members].
      Retrieved from https://static1.squarespace.com/
      static/5b198e03ee1759f2bea1054e/t/5cdaf69cee6eb0
      25aa6596b1/1557853869338/11737642-v1-2019-05-
      10+Letter+to+St.+Paul+City+Council.pdf

136   Office of the Minnesota Secretary of State. (n.d.).
      Twin Cities German Immersion School Building
      Company [Search engine result]. Retrieved July
      4, 2019, from https://mblsportal.sos.state.mn.us/
      Business/SearchDetails?filingGuid=2d882d2f-3b85-
      e411-ae63-001ec94ffe7f

137   Georgia Government Transparency and Campaign
      Finance Commission. (n.d.). Campaign reports: Name
      search [Search engine]. Retrieved from http://media.
      ethics.ga.gov/Search/Campaign/Campaign_ByName.
      aspx

138   Ballotpedia. (n.d.). Independent expenditure.
      Retrieved July 4, 2019, from https://ballotpedia.org/
      Independent_expenditure

139   Ballotpedia. (n.d.). Massachusetts authorization
      of additional charter schools and charter school
      expansion (2016). Retrieved July 4, 2019, from
      https://ballotpedia.org/Massachusetts_Authorization_
      of_Additional_Charter_Schools_and_Charter_
      School_Expansion,_Question_2_(2016)

140   Massachusetts Office of Campaign and Political
      Finance. (2016). Ballot question committee reports:
      Question 2 [Search engine result]. Retrieved from

https://www.ocpf.us/Reports/BallotQuestionReports

141 Massachusetts Office of Campaign and Political
     Finance. (2016). Ballot question committee
     reports: Question 2: Yes on 2 [Search engine
     result]. Retrieved from https://www.ocpf.us/Filers/
     Index?q=95436&section=Reports

142 Massachusetts Office of Campaign and Political
     Finance. (2016). Ballot question committee reports:
     Question 2 [Search engine result]. Retrieved from
     https://www.ocpf.us/Reports/BallotQuestionReports

143 Schneider, Mercedes K. (2016, September 10).
     Arkansas residents Jim and Alice Walton pony up
     $1,835,000 to raise charter cap in Massachusetts
     [Web blog post]. Retrieved from https://deutsch29.
     wordpress.com/2016/09/10/arkansas-residents-jim-
     and-alice-walton-pony-up-1835000-to-raise-charter-
     cap-in-massachusetts/

144 Massachusetts Office of Campaign and Political
     Finance. (2017, September 8). Disposition agreement
     between the Office of Campaign and Political
     Finance and Families for Excellent Schools Advocacy
     Committee. Retrieved from http://files.ocpf.us/pdf/
     actions/fesadafinal.pdf

145 Zimmerman, Alex, and Cramer, Philissa. (2018,
     February 5). Families for Excellent Schools says it
     will close, altering the education debate in New York.
     Chalkbeat. Retrieved from https://www.chalkbeat.org/
     posts/ny/2018/02/05/families-for-excellent-schools-
     may-close-altering-the-education-debate-in-new-
     york-city/

146 Zimmerman, Alex. (2018, January 31). Families for
     Excellent Schools CEO ousted after investigation
     into "inappropriate behavior." *Chalkbeat*. Retrieved
     from https://www.chalkbeat.org/posts/ny/2018/01/31/
     families-for-excellent-schools-ceo-ousted-after-
     investigation-into-inappropriate-behavior/

147 Ballotpedia. (n.d.). Massachusetts authorization
     of additional charter schools and charter school
     expansion (2016). Retrieved July 4, 2019, from
     https://ballotpedia.org/Massachusetts_Authorization_

of_Additional_Charter_Schools_and_Charter_
School_Expansion,_Question_2_(2016)

148 Louisiana Ethics Administration Program.
(2008). View campaign finance reports [Search
engine]. Retrieved from http://ethics.la.gov/
EthicsViewReports.aspx?Reports=CampaignFinance

149 Louisiana Board of Elementary and Secondary
Education. (n.d.). BESE member biographical
summary: Kira Orange-Jones, BESE District 2
representative. Retrieved July 4, 2019, from http://
bese.louisiana.gov/about-bese/bese's-district-2-
representative

150 Louisiana Ethics Administration Program. (n.d.).
Scanned reports for candidate: Jones, Kira Orange
(240389). Retrieved from http://www.ethics.la.gov/
CampaignFinanceSearch/ViewScannedFiler.
aspx?FilerID=240389

151 Louisiana Ethics Administration Program. (2011,
September 19). Candidate's report: Kira Orange
Jones. Retrieved from http://www.ethics.la.gov/
CampaignFinanceSearch/11004833.pdf

152 Louisiana Ethics Administration Program.
(2008). View campaign finance reports [Search
engine]. Retrieved from http://ethics.la.gov/
EthicsViewReports.aspx?Reports=CampaignFinance

153 Louisiana Ethics Administration Program. (n.d.).
Search electronically filed campaign finance
contributions [Search engine]. Retrieved from
http://www.ethics.la.gov/CampaignFinanceSearch/
SearchEfilingContributors.aspx

154 Louisiana Ethics Administration Program. (n.d.).
Search electronically filed campaign finance
contributions [Search engine]. Retrieved from
http://www.ethics.la.gov/CampaignFinanceSearch/
SearchEfilingContributors.aspx

155 Louisiana Ethics Administration Program. (2015,
November 12). L. Lane Grigsby, Chairman Empower
Louisiana, Inc., Political action committee [Search
engine result]. Retrieved from http://www.ethics.
la.gov/CampaignFinanceSearch/ShowEForm.

aspx?ReportID=54651

156 Louisiana Ethics Administration Program. (2015, October 14). L. Lane Grigsby, Chairman Empower Louisiana, Inc., Political action committee [Search engine result]. Retrieved from http://www.ethics. la.gov/CampaignFinanceSearch/ShowEForm. aspx?ReportID=52323

157 Louisiana Ethics Administration Program. (2016, February 16). L. Lane Grigsby, Chairman Empower Louisiana, Inc., Political action committee [Search engine result]. Retrieved from http://www.ethics. la.gov/CampaignFinanceSearch/ShowEForm. aspx?ReportID=57898

158 Ballotpedia. (n.d.). Louisiana Board of Elementary and Secondary Education. Retrieved June 2019 from https://ballotpedia.org/Louisiana_Board_of_ Elementary_and_Secondary_Education ; Schneider, Mercedes K. (2015, October 25). The billionaires bought BESE in 2015, but they didn't buy Edwards [Web blog post]. Retrieved from https://deutsch29. wordpress.com/2015/10/25/the-billionaires-bought-bese-in-2015-but-they-didnt-buy-edwards/

159 Schneider, Mercedes K. (2015, November 24). John White's employment contract [Web blog post]. Retrieved from https://deutsch29.wordpress. com/2015/11/24/john-whites-employment-contract/

160 Justia Dockets and Filings. (2019). Federal cases, dockets and filings from U.S. district courts and U.S. courts of appeal [Search engine]. Retrieved from https://dockets.justia.com/

161 Taylor, Kate. (2015, October 29). At a Success Academy charter school, singling out pupils who have "got to go." *The New York Times.* Retrieved from https://www.nytimes.com/2015/10/30/nyregion/ at-a-success-academy-charter-school-singling-out-pupils-who-have-got-to-go.html

162 United States District Court, Eastern District of New York. (2018, August 1). *Shawn Lawton et al. versus Success Academy Charter Schools, Inc. et al.* [Litigation]. Retrieved from https://www.govinfo.gov/

content/pkg/USCOURTS-nyed-1_15-cv-07058/pdf/
USCOURTS-nyed-1_15-cv-07058-0.pdf

163   Justia Dockets and Filings. (n.d.). Search for cases:
      Candido Brown [Search engine result]. Retrieved
      June 2019 from https://dockets.justia.com/search?part
      ies=candido+brown&cases=mostrecent&sort-by-last-
      update=false

164   Public Access to Court Electronic Records (PACER).
      (n.d.). Home page. Retrieved July 4, 2019, from
      https://www.pacer.gov/

165   PACER Individual Court Sites. (n.d.). Retrieved July
      4, 2019, from https://www.pacer.gov/psco/cgi-bin/
      links.pl

166   Justia US Law. (2019). Home page. Retrieved from
      https://law.justia.com/

167   Justia US Supreme Court. (2019). Us Supreme Court
      center. Retrieved from https://supreme.justia.com/

168   Justia US Law. (2019). Search results for:
      "Plessy." Retrieved from https://law.justia.com/
      lawsearch?query=plessy

169   Supreme Court of the United States. (n.d.). Opinions
      of the Court—2018 and prior [Index]. Retrieved
      July 4, 2019, from https://www.supremecourt.gov/
      opinions/slipopinion/18

170   Supreme Court of the United States. (n.d.). Case
      citation finder [Search engine]. Retrieved July 4,
      2019, from https://www.supremecourt.gov/opinions/
      casefinder.aspx

171   Glassdoor. (2019). Home page. Retrieved from
      https://www.glassdoor.com/

172   Glassdoor. (2019). Success Academy Charter
      Schools: School reviews [Search engine result].
      Retrieved June 29, 2019, from https://www.glassdoor.
      com/Reviews/Success-Academy-Charter-Schools-
      Reviews-E381408_P4.htm

173   Chicago Public Schools. (2019). Freedom of
      Information Act (FOIA) requests. Retrieved from
      https://cps.edu/About_CPS/Departments/Law/Pages/
      FOIARequest.aspx

174 U.S. Department of Justice Office of Information Policy. (n.d.) What is FOIA? Retrieved June 30, 2019, from https://www.foia.gov/about.html

175 National Center for Education Statistics. (n.d.). Data tools. Retrieved June 30, 2019, from https://nces. ed.gov/datatools/

176 National Center for Education Statistics. (n.d.). Cohort graduation rate [Search engine result]. Retrieved June 30, 2019, from https://nces.ed.gov/sea rch/?q=cohort+graduation+rate

177 Center for Education Statistics. (n.d.). Trends in high school dropout and completion rates in the United States. Retrieved June 30, 2019, from https://nces. ed.gov/programs/dropout/ind_05.asp

178 Schneider, Mercedes K. (2019, February 2). Lycée Français de la Nouvelle-Orléans: Still too white [Web blog post]. Retrieved from https://deutsch29. wordpress.com/2019/02/02/lycee-francais-de-la-nouvelle-orleans-still-too-white/

179 Louisiana Department of Education. (n.d.) Student attributes. Retrieved July 4, 2019, from https://www. louisianabelieves.com/resources/library/student-attributes

180 Schneider, Mercedes K. (2019, February 2). Lycée Français de la Nouvelle-Orléans: Still too white [Web blog post]. Retrieved from https://deutsch29. wordpress.com/2019/02/02/lycee-francais-de-la-nouvelle-orleans-still-too-white/

181 Chen, James. (2018, March 24). Earnings call. *Investopedia.* Retrieved from https://www. investopedia.com/terms/e/earnings-call.asp

182 Seeking Alpha. (2014, February 28). Pearson management discusses 2013 results—earnings call transcript. Retrieved from https://seekingalpha.com/ article/2058743-pearson-management-discusses-2013-results-earnings-call-transcript

183 Seeking Alpha. (2019). Home page. Retrieved July 4, 2019, from https://seekingalpha.com/

184 Schneider, Mercedes K. (2014, May 20). Pearson

allows me to quote 400 board meeting words [Web blog post]. Retrieved from https://deutsch29. wordpress.com/2014/05/20/pearson-allows-me-to-quote-400-board-meeting-words/

185   Schneider, Mercedes K. (2015). Those "Powerful market Forces": Pearson Wins [Book chapter]. In *Common Core Dilemma: Who Owns Our Schools?* New York: Teachers College Press.

186   Partnership for Assessment of Readiness for College and Careers (2019, July 18). License and participation models [Archived web page]. Retrieved from https:// web.archive.org/web/20190718225813/https://parcc-assessment.org/license-participation-models/

187   Partnership for Assessment of Readiness for College and Careers (2019, July 18). About [Archived web page]. Retrieved from https://web.archive.org/ web/20190718160950/https://parcc-assessment.org/ about/

188   Network for Public Education. (2018). 2018 National Conference [Archived conference program]. Retrieved from https://networkforpubliceducation. org/2018-national-conference/

189   Cimarusti, Darcie; Gabor, Andrea, and Schneider, Mercedes. (2018, October 21). Where did all this money come from?? Locating and following the dark money trail [Presentation]. Network for Public Education 2018 conference. Retrieved from https://networkforpubliceducation.org/wp-content/ uploads/2019/01/Where-Did-All-of-this-Money-Come-From-min.pdf

ABOUT THE AUTHOR

Mercedes K. Schneider, Ph.D., began blogging on educational reform issues in 2013 at *deutsch29.wordpress.com*. She quickly became a trusted source for data-based analysis of the most provocative issues in education. Schneider has gained a national readership, including educators and scholars in multiple fields, because her blog posts are data-based and fact-checked, and she reaches conclusions and makes bold statements that others who have not analyzed the data cannot make. She is quintessentially one of the best in the field.

Schneider has previously authored three books, all concerning education reform issues: *A Chronicle of Echoes: Who's Who in the Implosion of American Public Education* (2014, Information Age Press); *Common Core Dilemma: Who Owns Our Schools?* (2015, TC Press), and *School Choice: The End of Public Education?* (2016, TC Press).

She holds degrees in secondary English and German (B.S., Louisiana State, 1991), guidance and counseling (M.Ed., West Georgia, 1998), and applied statistics and research methods (Ph.D.,

Northern Colorado, 2002). She is an unwavering advocate for public education and teaches high school in her native southern Louisiana. Her 27-year teaching career involves 24 full-time years teaching public school (19 years) and post-secondary (5 years).

INDEX

H

Haycock, Kati 25
Horstman, Molly 37, 38

I

interview 1, 8, 10, 11, 24, 50, 51, 52, 54, 55, 56, 57, 58, 59,
       60, 61, 62, 63
IRS 82, 83, 84, 96, 97

J

Justia 9, 111, 112, 113

K

Katherine Westerhold 43
keyword 14, 17, 18, 39, 41, 44, 46, 48, 81, 85, 95, 101, 102,
       110, 112, 118
Klein, Joel 18
Kockler, Rebecca 45

L

LDOE 21, 22, 37, 39, 43, 44, 45, 119, 120
legal name 35
litigation 8, 9, 111
LLC 89, 96, 98, 99, 100
Louisiana Department of Education 21, 37, 42, 117, 119

M

Max and Marjorie Fisher Foundation 79, 80
Morris, Ted 40, 41
Moskowitz, Eva 16, 17, 18, 19, 92, 93

N

National Center for Education Statistics 118
NCES 118
Network for Public Education 125
New Orleans 51, 52, 53, 59, 75, 99, 118, 119

Made in the USA
Middletown, DE
08 November 2020

23522519R00096